CQ, Cultural Education as a Framework for Policy Formation

Shaping Inclusive Societies with Sensitivity, Awareness and Responsiveness

By **Dr Jamel Kaur Singh**

Adapted from her Thesis with
Edmonton University
under the supervision of
Dr Thivagharan Nair

Dedication

Waheguru Ji's blessings, to my Dad, Dya Singh, for his ongoing support, motivation and inspiration. For constantly reminding to find my 'ikigai'.

Published by Consultsingh
PO Box 77, Doveton, 3177, Australia

First Published June 2025

www.CulturalEducation.com.au

Author: Jamel Kaur Singh
Cover Illustrator: Ronald Santos
Inspired & approved by
Uncle Gene Blow
Editors: Jamel Kaur Singh, Dya Singh &
Johanna Marie Ferrer

ISBN 978-0-9756100-7-7

Produced by Consultsingh Pty. Ltd.

Story About the Cover Design

Totemic Life and Its Lessons for Cultural Education

Totemic life within First Nations communities embodies the profound connection between environment, spirituality, and social responsibility. This way of life is grounded in four key categories: land, sky, water, and spirit. These totems are not merely symbols; they are integral to an individual's identity and role within their community, offering purpose and fostering interconnectedness from the earliest stages of life.

A totem is traditionally bestowed at birth or during the early stages of adolescence, marking the individual's connection to the world around them. For example, a totem may be inspired by an animal that has a significant presence in one's life, either in dreams or in reality. In some traditions, the midwifes may assign a totem at birth, with a portion of the afterbirth buried at a tree, symbolising the child's responsibility to care for and nurture that tree throughout their life. This act roots the individual to their land and heritage, instilling a sense of duty and purpose from the very beginning.

Totemic life is integral to the social structure of First Nations communities. It governs relationships, including marriage, ensuring cultural and genetic diversity by requiring individuals to marry outside their own totem. This system strengthens the community by preventing inbreeding and fostering alliances across clans. Through the *"kippa-ring"* (coming-of-age ceremony), young men transition into adulthood, taking on new responsibilities, including the potential to marry and contribute to the broader cultural and spiritual ecosystem.

The cyclical nature of Totemic life extends to the community's broader sustainability practices. Gatherings,

3

represented in the title cover artwork, are symbolic of the meeting of communities for ceremonial, social, and economic purposes. These gatherings, often marked by corroboree (dance and storytelling), serve as spaces to exchange tools, medicines, laws, and stories, as well as to strengthen intercommunity relationships, including marriages. The pathways depicted in the design converge into a central circle, symbolising the "council"—a collective coming together to establish objectives and chart a sustainable future for all.

This profound system, rooted in balance and mutual respect, aligns deeply with the principles of Cultural Education. Just as Totemic life emphasises interconnectedness, responsibility, and shared knowledge, Cultural Education aims to foster empathy, dismantle biases, and create inclusive societies. Both frameworks highlight the importance of acknowledging and honouring diverse perspectives for the collective well-being and sustainability of communities.

Uncle Gene Blow
Koonarang Noonuccal
Koonarang is my totem (ringtail Possum) and Noonuccal is my mob on Straddie. This is how I was named after going through my Kippa-Ring.

The artwork for the book cover by Ronald Santos, has been inspired by Uncle Gene. It beautifully encapsulates these themes, offering a visual representation of unity, diversity, and the power of collaboration. It is a reminder of the enduring wisdom within First Nations practices and their relevance to modern societal challenges - a perfect complement to the transformative insights explored in *Cultural Education as a Framework for Policy Formation.*

Table of Contents

Preface

In an increasingly interconnected world, cultural diversity stands as both a challenge and a strength. CQ, **Cultural Education as a Framework for Self & Policy Formation** explores how **Cultural Education**, beginning in infancy, serves as a transformative tool to cultivate empathy, reduce biases, and create equitable and cohesive societies. At its heart, Cultural Education is the pathway to developing **Cultural Intelligence (CQ)** - the ability to navigate cultural complexities with sensitivity, awareness, and responsiveness.

Cultural Intelligence (CQ) equips individuals and organisations to work effectively across diverse cultural contexts, bridging divides and fostering mutual understanding. This book positions Cultural Education as the foundation for CQ, empowering societies to address systemic inequities, embrace diversity, and build a collective sense of belonging.

This book delves into Cultural Education's transformative potential across three critical domains:

1. **Policy Development**
   Cultural Education - and the CQ it fosters - lays the groundwork for inclusive and equitable policies. By embedding cultural awareness into early education, policymakers can build a foundation for societal cohesion and equity. This approach ensures that public policies reflect the diversity of the population, tackling systemic biases at their roots.
2. **Corporate Success**
   Organisations that prioritise inclusivity experience enhanced innovation, access to broader talent pools, and improved employee retention.

Developing CQ through Cultural Education reshapes workplace dynamics, aligning with the triple bottom line of people, planet, and profit, while promoting a psychologically safe environment.

3. **Social Cohesion**
Early education shapes societal attitudes and behaviours. By addressing biases from the outset, Cultural Education fosters Cultural Intelligence, cultivating a generation that values empathy, respect, and inclusion, creating a more harmonious society.

Australia's journey from a pristine ancient **Dreamtime**, a country of First Nations with their own laws and lores, through to a white invasion and the resultant **White Australia** policy, to an emerging multicultural society demonstrates the significance of cultural understanding. However, persistent stereotypes, biases, and exclusionary practices signal the need for institutional change. Current global challenges, including rising anti-Semitism and Islamophobia, further underscore the urgency for action. This book provides actionable insights to leverage Cultural Education and CQ as tools for shaping inclusive policies and practices.

CQ, Cultural Education as a Framework for Self & Policy Formation envisions Cultural Education - and CQ - as catalysts for societal transformation. By equipping individuals, governments, educators, and corporations with the tools to embrace diversity, it advocates for a more inclusive, empathetic, and prosperous future. This book is not just an academic endeavour but a persistent call to action, urging stakeholders at every level to invest in Cultural Education and CQ as the foundation for not only a better Australia but a better world.

Introduction

The Imperative of Cultural Education in a Globalised World

In an era of unprecedented global connectivity, cultural diversity is not merely a characteristic of modern societies - it is their essence. Yet, despite the rich tapestry of traditions, languages, and perspectives that define humanity, biases, stereotypes, and systemic inequities persist, creating barriers to true inclusion and equity. Cultural Education offers a transformative framework to address these challenges, serving as a foundation for uniting communities, shaping inclusive policies, and preparing societies for a shared, equitable future.

As societies drift further from traditional religious practices and the community structures they often provide, we find ourselves grappling with the loss of shared ethical frameworks - those universal teachings of values, morals, and purpose that transcend individual belief systems. Without these grounding principles, we risk losing not only a sense of belonging but also the mental health benefits that faith communities have historically offered, such as mindfulness, visualisation, and connection to a higher purpose. Cultural Education steps in to fill this gap, offering a secular yet deeply ethical lens through which we can navigate the complexities of our globalised world.

Cultural Intelligence (CQ): The Cornerstone of Cultural Education

At its core, **Cultural Intelligence (CQ)** is the ability to relate to and work effectively across cultures. It encompasses the sensitivity, awareness, and responsiveness necessary to navigate diverse environments with empathy and respect. Throughout this book, the term **Cultural Education** serves as the practical and educational application of CQ, equipping individuals and organisations to develop the skills, knowledge, and mindset essential for thriving in a multicultural world.

CQ is built on four key dimensions:
1. **Drive** – The motivation to engage with other cultures and navigate diversity.
2. **Knowledge** – Understanding cultural norms, values, and practices.
3. **Strategy** – The ability to plan and adjust in cross-cultural interactions.
4. **Action** – Effectively adapting behaviour to align with different cultural contexts.

These dimensions mirror the objectives of Cultural Education as outlined in this book. By fostering CQ, Cultural Education transforms individuals and institutions, enabling them to bridge divides, challenge prejudices, and create spaces for mutual understanding.

In essence, CQ is the skillset, and Cultural Education is the pathway to developing it. Together, they provide a cohesive framework for shaping inclusive policies, educational strategies, and organisational practices. As you read through this book, you will see how the principles of CQ underpin every facet of Cultural Education, offering actionable insights for creating societies that celebrate diversity, equity, and inclusion.

A Cradle-to-Grave Approach
Cultural Education must be a lifelong journey, a "cradle-to-grave" approach that begins in early childhood and continues through every stage of life. From the stories shared with toddlers that shape their understanding of diversity, to the workplace initiatives that challenge biases, to the elder wisdom that fosters intergenerational dialogue, Cultural Education evolves alongside us. This comprehensive approach ensures that individuals, organisations, and societies remain attuned to the shifting dynamics of culture, equity, and inclusion.

At its core, Cultural Education is about more than imparting knowledge of customs or traditions. It is a transformative tool that shapes empathy, challenges biases, and cultivates shared humanity. It bridges the gaps in understanding that perpetuate prejudice and fosters a sense of belonging that is vital for mental and emotional well-being.

Objectives of Cultural Education
This book highlights the transformative role of Cultural Education in shaping inclusive societies through sensitivity, awareness, and responsiveness. The core objectives are:
1. **Fostering Empathy and Understanding**: Empowering individuals to appreciate diverse perspectives and histories, cultivating shared humanity.
2. **Enhancing Awareness of Diversity**: Raising consciousness about cultural richness and addressing systemic inequities.
3. **Equipping for Intercultural Communication**: Providing tools for engaging respectfully and effectively in multicultural environments.

4. **Encouraging Critical Thinking**: Inspiring individuals to examine biases and power structures critically, nurturing an inclusive mindset.
5. **Creating Shared Spaces for Dialogue**: Building platforms for open conversations on identity, belonging, and inclusion.
6. **Promoting Ethical Frameworks and Belonging**: Addressing the societal void left by the decline of traditional religious communities, offering alternative frameworks for moral and social cohesion.

Australia as a Case Study: Lessons for the World
Australia's multicultural journey - marked by waves of migration, cultural evolution, and persistent challenges - offers a compelling narrative for understanding the promises and complexities of diversity. From combating anti-Semitism and Islamophobia to addressing cultural siloing, Australia's experience is both a cautionary tale and a source of inspiration. By examining its successes and challenges alongside global best practices, this book provides a blueprint for building empathy, inclusivity, and societal harmony that resonates far beyond Australia's borders.

A Personal Journey of Cultural Advocacy
As the daughter of internationally renowned musician and author, Dya Singh and interfaith and peace advocate, Jessiee Kaur Singh, my life has been a symphony of cultural exchange and spiritual dialogue. My father's music, blending Sikh devotional hymns with global influences, became a bridge between traditions and a celebration of shared humanity. On stages around the world, my family represented Australia's multicultural ethos, collaborating with artists from diverse traditions and showcasing the beauty of unity through diversity.

At home, my parents' work in interfaith dialogue and community building instilled in me the values of empathy, respect, and cultural understanding. By the age of eleven, I was immersed in interfaith discussions, taking minutes at meetings of leaders from diverse traditions who came together to address shared challenges with the Multifaith Association of South Australia which my parents formulated in the late 1980s. These experiences shaped my belief in the power of Cultural Education to transform lives and societies.

A Vision for the Future
Cultural Education is not merely a subject to be taught; it is an ethos to be lived. It bridges the gaps in understanding that perpetuate prejudice, fosters a sense of belonging essential to mental and emotional well-being, and provides the ethical framework necessary for navigating an increasingly interconnected world.

This book invites policymakers, educators, corporate leaders, and individuals to embark on a journey of self-reflection. It challenges readers to confront their biases, examine their sense of belonging, and consider how Cultural Education can be a tool for building a more harmonious society. By embedding these principles into foundational courses, workplace strategies, and public policy, we can equip individuals and institutions to embrace diversity with sensitivity, awareness, and responsiveness.

As the world grows more interconnected yet divided, the urgency for Cultural Education - and the Cultural Intelligence (CQ) it fosters - has never been clearer. Together, they are a necessity for creating inclusive, equitable, and sustainable societies. Through this book, we can lay the groundwork for a future where diversity is not just acknowledged but celebrated - a world where every individual feels valued, every community thrives, and every voice is heard.

Chapter 1
Defining Cultural Education

Cultural Education transcends the simple teaching of customs or traditions. It is an immersive process that instils awareness, sensitivity, and acceptance of diverse identities from the earliest stages of life.

What is Culture?

Culture is the essence of who we are as individuals and as communities. It is both the invisible thread that connects people within a group, and the distinguishing mark that sets one group apart from another. While a dictionary might describe culture as the ideas, customs, and social behaviours of a particular people or society, this definition barely scratches the surface of its profound significance.

Culture encompasses language, dress, art, values, religion, beliefs, attitudes, food, music, stories/lore, dance, and song. It is both tangible and intangible, encompassing the practices we engage in and the underlying beliefs that guide our behaviours. Culture is what makes us the same and different from someone else; it is simultaneously a mirror and a mosaic.

For example, some people take off their shoes before entering a house, while others do not. Some families sit around a dining table for dinner, while others eat casually on the couch. These small practices are cultural markers that are not inherently good or bad - they are just simply different.

Australian Culture: A Unique Blend

Defining what it means to be Australian is a complex task. Australia is a nation built on layers of culture: from the ancient and enduring cultures of First Nations people to the colonial influences of Britain, and then the vibrant multiculturalism brought by successive influxes of migrants from across the seas.

At its heart, Australian culture values **mateship** - the idea of looking out for your neighbour, lending a helping hand, and encouraging a spirit of camaraderie. This is paired with a 'glass-half-full' approach to life, an optimism and resilience that has come to define the Australian psyche.

Australians are also deeply passionate about sport, which serves as a unifying force across diverse communities. Whether it is cricket, AFL, soccer, netball or swimming, sport embodies values of fairness, teamwork, and perseverance.

Being Australian today means embracing diversity. It means recognising that our national identity is enriched by the many languages, traditions, and beliefs of the people who call this country home.

Integration versus Assimilation

Understanding the difference between integration and assimilation is key to advancing inclusivity. **Integration:** Encourages newcomers to retain their cultural identities while adapting to Australian norms of shared national ethos. **Assimilation:** Demands the relinquishment of cultural distinctiveness to conform to the dominant culture. Cultural Education must emphasise integration as a pathway to social cohesion. Which is what Australia has already experienced in the throwback to the 'White Australia Policy', especially to the First Nations people. Assimilation devastated and weakened them through which they still have not recovered.

Personal Experiences: A Campaign of Bias and Belonging

In September 2024, I made the decision to stand as a candidate for Local Council, in the City of Casey. As a Sikh woman and a first-generation migrant, I wanted to bring my lived experience to the table. However, my campaign quickly became a microcosm of the biases and stereotypes this book aims to address.

My corflute boards were defaced with the words "Australia is for Australians," an act of racial vilification that not only hurt me personally but also served as a stark reminder of the work that remains in building an inclusive society. Media coverage of the incident amplified the message that racism persists, even in communities that pride themselves on multiculturalism.

During the campaign, I was also struck by comments such as, "Oh, you speak 'Australian' really well," from individuals who assumed, based on my appearance or name, that I was 'from here.' These remarks revealed both conscious and unconscious biases and underscored how deeply ingrained stereotypes shape perceptions.

My gender also played a role in the controversy. As the only woman among the candidates in my ward, I faced scrutiny that my male counterparts did not, including from them, (which became very apparent during the preferencing), highlighting the intersectionality of race and gender in public discourse. One of the main candidates also promoted himself (after I started my campaign) as the "genuine local" candidate to which even rational thinking, well-meaning Anglo Saxon folk could not understand why that was racially harmful, especially seeing we had both lived in the City of Casey for the same number of years!

This experience was not just a test of resilience - it was a real-world research for this book. It illuminated how biases are formed, perpetuated, and challenged, and it reinforced the need for Cultural Education to dismantle stereotypes and build understanding.

Demystifying Culture and Its Role in Society

Culture is often perceived as something exotic or foreign - an 'otherness' to be observed from the outside. However, culture is neither distant nor abstract; it is the fabric of everyday life. Each school, workplace, sports club, and community has its own culture, defined by shared values, practices, and goals.

For example:
- A school's culture might prioritise inclusivity, innovation, or academic excellence. They have their own dress code, language(s) spoken, art, dance, and sporting culture.
- A sports club might be built around teamwork, competition, or community engagement.
- A business might aim to instil a culture of creativity, customer focus, or diversity, equity, and inclusion (DEI).

The challenge lies in ensuring that these cultural goals are not just aspirational but actively implemented. A DEI policy, for instance, is meaningless unless accompanied by genuine efforts to embed inclusivity into daily practices. It requires standing firm on core values and holding individuals accountable to those principles.

The Role of Cultural Education in Policy and Society

Cultural Education is the process of teaching and learning about the diverse cultural identities that make up our world. It demystifies culture, promoting an understanding that cultural differences are not barriers but bridges to connection.

In the context of schools, Cultural Education equips students with the skills to navigate a diverse world. By learning about different traditions, languages, and histories, students develop empathy, curiosity, and a sense of global citizenship. Parents and teachers play a vital role in instilling these values, shaping young minds to embrace diversity as a strength.

In a national context, Cultural Education can promote social cohesion by helping individuals understand the difference between assimilation and integration (which will be expanded in Chapter 7). Integration celebrates diversity within a unified national identity, while assimilation demands conformity at the expense of heritage. By emphasising integration, Cultural Education builds pride in Australia's multicultural fabric while sustaining a shared commitment to common values (expanded in Chapter 7).

In 2009, the Parliament of the World's Religions convened in Melbourne, and my mother played a pivotal role in bringing this prestigious event to Australia. I had the honour of being part of the organising team at Cultural Infusion, overseeing the daily events in the atrium and serving as both the Master of Ceremonies and

Voice-over artist for the proceedings. This experience was a masterclass in cultural and spiritual education, offering me the unique opportunity to interact with faith leaders from around the globe, including the Dalai Lama, Sri Sri Ravi Shankar, Bhai Mohinder Singh, Father Jeff Foale, Dadi Janki, and others whose wisdom transcended their religious traditions.

A pivotal moment for me was facilitating the inclusion and respect for First Nations communities within the event. Their voices and cultural practices were woven into the fabric of the Parliament, empowering them to take centre stage in an international forum. This experience underscored the profound impact of 'holding space' where all cultures and faiths feel valued and heard. It was a testament to how Cultural Education, when practised intentionally, develops environments of respect, understanding, and empowerment.

The Psychology of Cultural Development

Cultural Education begins in the earliest stages of life, shaping perceptions, attitudes, and behaviours that persist into adulthood. Research shows that by the age of three, children are already developing social awareness and forming ideas about themselves and others based on the cues they receive from their environment. These early impressions are pivotal, as they can either entrench prejudices or create a foundation of open-mindedness and acceptance, yet reinforcing pride in one's own background and consciousness.

Existing research

Existing research, such as Smith's *Cultural Responsiveness: A Conceptual Model for Mental Health Professionals Engaging with Aboriginal and Torres*

Strait Islander People, has laid essential groundwork in understanding cultural responsiveness in specific contexts like mental health. Similarly, initiatives like the CICRTool address embedded inequities in social work education. This publication builds on these contributions by broadening the scope to explore Cultural Education as a transformative framework for shaping policy and strengthening societal cohesion across multiple domains.

Early Childhood Influence

Home environments and early learning settings play a crucial role in shaping a child's understanding of diversity. The interactions children have with their parents, caregivers, and peers provide their first exposure to cultural norms and values. When children are encouraged to explore differences - such as hearing multiple languages at home, celebrating diverse traditions, or reading books that showcase a variety of cultures - they develop empathy and a broader worldview. Conversely, environments that lack diversity or reinforce stereotypes can lead to the formation of biases that are difficult to undo later in life.

Educators and parents have an opportunity to intervene positively during these formative years by 'holding space' where curiosity about diversity is celebrated. Simple practices, such as introducing children to culturally diverse toys, foods, or stories, can spark lifelong curiosity and understanding. Programs like cultural storytelling or art-based learning initiatives provide immersive ways to engage young learners in appreciating the world's richness.

Role of Media and Representation

The media consumed by children - whether books, television, or online content - profoundly influences their understanding of cultural identities. Positive representation in media is essential, as it provides children with role models who reflect a range of experiences, appearances, and abilities.

For example, children who see characters of diverse backgrounds working together in cartoons or hear multilingual characters in books learn to see inclusivity as normal. Conversely, the absence of representation - or worse, the perpetuation of negative stereotypes - can reinforce societal biases. Ensuring that media portrays accurate, respectful, and positive depictions of different cultures is a powerful way to counteract prejudice and steer from exclusion, racism and fear of misunderstanding.

Education as an Intervention

Schools are uniquely positioned to serve as intervention points where cultural biases can be addressed and replaced with empathy and understanding. Curricula that prioritise inclusivity teach children not only about different cultures but also about the importance of respect and equity. Programs like cultural awareness weeks, language immersion, and historical education about First Nations peoples and other cultural groups provide students with tangible, meaningful experiences that challenge stereotypes.

A critical component of this process is the ability of teachers to 'hold space' for their students. Originating from psychological frameworks and popularised by Heather Plett, 'holding space' refers to being fully present and creating an environment where individuals feel safe to express themselves without fear of judgment. In the classroom, this means teachers must be physically, mentally, and emotionally present, actively listening to their students, validating their experiences, and guiding discussions with empathy and compassion. By holding space, educators not only model inclusivity but also cultivate a psychologically safe environment where challenging conversations about diversity and bias can occur constructively.

The research initiative *Toward an Australian Culturally Responsive Pedagogy* by Morrison et al. underscores the importance of equipping educators with cultural competency and the skills to hold space effectively. When teachers are trained to manage diverse classrooms with sensitivity, they transform their classrooms into microcosms of an inclusive society, reinforcing this book's ultimate goal of infusing Cultural Education into national curricula as a foundation for building societal cohesion from early childhood.

Cultural Sensitivity in the Classroom

An anecdote that highlights the importance of cultural awareness in education occurred during a school sports day I attended in Melbourne. A well-meaning teacher handed out snacks at the event. Unintentionally, she offered beef jerky to a Hindu student and pork sausages as part of the BBQ to a Muslim student. Both children declined politely but were visibly uncomfortable. Later, a Sikh student was proudly showing off his medal, only to have the teacher instinctively reach out and pat the student's head - a gesture that is deeply disrespectful in Sikhism, where the hair and head are considered sacred. The 'patka' (a small turban worn by children) should only be touched by those helping with their hair or assisting them to fix it.

These incidents were not born of malice but stemmed from a lack of cultural awareness, underscoring the need for educators to be equipped with cultural knowledge. Teachers who understand the diverse traditions, dietary practices, and values of their students can create an environment of mutual respect. This isn't about isolating students into cultural silos but ensuring that classrooms are inclusive spaces where all students feel acknowledged, respected, and supported.

A particularly nuanced issue arises in schools where canteens adopt halal-certified meat to accommodate Muslim students. While this initiative reflects a commendable effort to cater to diverse needs, it can unintentionally create challenges for other communities. For example, Sikh students are prohibited from consuming halal meat due to religious doctrines that view the method of preparation as inhumane. This approach, while aimed at inclusivity, can inadvertently exclude or alienate others who feel their own values are being overlooked.

Such policies, though well-intentioned, can also contribute to broader societal tensions. By focusing on one group's dietary requirements without considering the full spectrum of cultural needs, schools risk stimulating feelings of resentment or perceptions of favouritism. This dynamic can inadvertently deepen misunderstandings and breed divisions, particularly when people perceive these changes as an imposition rather than an inclusive solution.

To navigate these complexities, schools must adopt a holistic approach to cultural sensitivity, ensuring that decisions are made with input from all communities. This collaborative effort can help mitigate unintended consequences while cultivating an environment of respect and mutual understanding. Inclusivity is not about privileging one group over another but about creating equitable solutions that respect and accommodate the diversity of the entire student body.

Lifelong Cultural Learning

Cultural Education does not end in childhood; it is a lifelong journey that evolves as individuals encounter new experiences and challenges. The stages of life present distinct opportunities for deepening cultural understanding and progressing inclusivity.

Adolescence and Identity Formation

During adolescence, individuals grapple with questions of identity and belonging, making this a critical period for Cultural Education. Teenagers are heavily influenced by their social groups, which can either reinforce inclusivity or amplify biases.

Cultural Education at this stage must focus on empowering adolescents to appreciate their own identities while respecting the identities of others. The concept of 'holding space' for them is critical. Initiatives such as exchange programs, multicultural student clubs, and service-learning projects expose teenagers to diverse perspectives, encouraging them to view differences as opportunities for growth rather than division.

Adult Education and Workplace Training

For adults, Cultural Education often intersects with professional development. As workplaces become more diverse, cultural competency training 'Cultural Responsiveness', has emerged as a vital framework for facilitating collaboration, reducing discrimination, and enhancing productivity.

Effective training goes beyond surface-level discussions of diversity to address unconscious biases and systemic inequalities. For example, workplace programs might explore scenarios where cultural misunderstandings lead to conflict, providing employees with strategies to navigate these challenges constructively. When leaders champion Cultural Education and model inclusive practices, they set a tone that permeates the organisation and creates a culture of respect and belonging.

Community Engagement

Beyond individual learning, Cultural Education thrives in communal spaces where people can come together to share stories, traditions, and experiences. Events like interfaith dialogues, multicultural festivals, and community storytelling nights provide opportunities for individuals to connect across cultural divides.

Participating in such events enhances empathy and understanding on a societal level. When adults engage in Cultural Education within their communities, they not only enrich their own lives but also contribute to a more cohesive, harmonious society. This ripple effect ensures that Cultural Education extends beyond institutions and into the fabric of everyday life.

Building Bridges through Cultural Education

The ultimate goal of Cultural Education is to build bridges - between communities, between individuals, and between the past, present and the future. It is a framework for societal change, creating social cohesion and reducing divisiveness.

By understanding and appreciating the cultures around us, we can move beyond stereotypes and biases to form meaningful connections. This requires a shift in pedagogy and methodology, embedding Cultural Education into curricula, workplaces, and community programs.

Policies that prioritise Cultural Education must go beyond tokenistic gestures. They should include:
- Comprehensive training for educators and leaders in Cultural Responsiveness.
- Representation of diverse voices in decision-making processes.
- Resources that celebrate and amplify marginalised cultures.

Conclusion: Culture as the Foundation of Inclusivity

Culture is not static; it is dynamic and ever-evolving. It shapes how we see ourselves and how we interact with the world. By investing in Cultural Education, we can create a society where differences are celebrated rather than feared, and where every individual feels a sense of belonging.

Chapter 2
Australia's Immigration Waves and Cultural Policy

Australia's cultural landscape has been profoundly shaped by successive waves of immigration, each contributing to the nation's evolving identity. This chapter examines the historical progression of immigration policies and their cultural implications, highlighting key legislative actions and the leaders who championed them.

The First Nations Peoples of Australia: A Rich Cultural Legacy

Before European settlement, the Australian continent was home to more than 300 distinct First Nations groups, often referred to as "mobs." Each mob represented a unique cultural and social identity, with its own language, traditions, and systems of governance. These communities thrived for tens of thousands of years, developing complex ways of life deeply connected to the land and their spiritual beliefs.

First Nations peoples spoke over 250 languages, encompassing more than 800 dialects. These languages were not only a means of communication but also vessels of knowledge, lore, and sacred stories known as the Dreamtime. The Dreamtime narratives, central to First Nations spirituality, explained the origins of the world, moral codes, and the connection between people, land, and ancestors. Dreamtime stories were passed down through oral traditions, dances, songs, and art, creating a rich tapestry of culture that guided daily life (AIATSIS 2023).

Art styles, ceremonies, and practices varied significantly across the continent, reflecting the diverse landscapes and environments that shaped each mob's way of life. The connection to the land was not merely utilitarian but deeply spiritual. The land was viewed as a living entity, imbued with ancestral spirits, and central to community identity. This profound relationship underpinned their seasonal movements, sustainable hunting practices, and resource management, ensuring ecological balance for generations.

The arrival of Europeans in 1788 disrupted this intricate cultural fabric, initiating a period of profound loss and upheaval for First Nations peoples (NLA 2024).

Early European Exploration and Indigenous Impact

The recorded European presence in Australia began in 1606 when Dutch navigator Willem Janszoon landed on the western side of Cape York Peninsula aboard the *Duyfken*. While Janszoon's exploration marked the first documented European contact, it did not lead to immediate colonisation or long-term European settlement.

The most transformative period of European exploration came more than 150 years later with British navigator Captain James Cook. In 1770, Cook sailed along the east coast of Australia aboard the *Endeavour*, charting the coastline and claiming the territory for Britain under the name "New South Wales." Cook's expedition, particularly his landing at Botany Bay, is often credited with laying the groundwork for Britain's eventual colonisation of the continent. His voyage was not merely exploratory but strategic, aimed at asserting British presence in the Pacific and assessing the viability of establishing settlements.

Eighteen years after Cook's voyage, the British First Fleet arrived in 1788 under the leadership of Captain Arthur Phillip. The fleet, comprising of eleven ships, brought over 700 convicts, guards, and their families to establish a penal colony at Port Jackson, now Sydney. Between 1788 and 1868, more than 162,000 convicts were transported to Australia, with penal colonies established in various locations across the continent. These settlements addressed Britain's overcrowded prisons and served as a mechanism to assert imperial dominance in the Pacific, expanding its influence in a geopolitically strategic region.

Over time, free settlers began to arrive, attracted by the promise of land and economic opportunities. This influx marked the beginning of widespread land appropriation and displacement of First Nations peoples. The British justified their colonisation through the doctrine of '*terra nullius*', declaring the land "nobody's land" (NLA 2024). This concept ignored the sophisticated societies and governance systems already in place, paving the way for dispossession and marginalisation.

The effects of British colonisation on First Nations communities were catastrophic. Frontier wars erupted as First Nations peoples resisted the encroachment on their lands, but these conflicts were overwhelmingly one-sided due to disparities in weaponry and resources. Alongside violence, the introduction of European diseases decimated Indigenous populations, who had no immunity to illnesses such as smallpox and influenza.

Genocide and Cultural Erasure

The British colonisation of Australia resulted in what many historians and advocates describe as acts of genocide. This included massacres of First Nations peoples, forced removals from ancestral lands, and the destruction of cultural practices. The use of terms such as "full blood," "half-caste," and "quarter-caste" reflected a dehumanising approach to categorising Indigenous people, often used to justify policies of control and exclusion.

The doctrine of racial superiority underpinning these policies extended to efforts to assimilate First Nations peoples into white society. Authorities established missions and reserves where mobs were torn apart and confined, subjected to strict regulations. These spaces were intended to "civilise the Indigenous people" by erasing their cultural identities and enforcing European ways of life (Attwood 2005).

The Stolen Generations

Perhaps the most devastating legacy of Australia's assimilation policies was the forced removal of First Nations children from their families. This practice, which spanned from the late 19th century to the 1970s, is now known as the 'Stolen Generation' (Reynolds 2006).

Under government policies, children were taken from their families and placed in institutions or raised by white families. The aim was to sever their ties to their communities and raise them as "White Australians". This involved changing their names, prohibiting the use of their languages, and denying them access to their Dreamtime stories and cultural practices.

The psychological, cultural, and emotional impact of these removals was profound. For many children, it meant a loss of identity and connection to their heritage. For parents and communities, it was a source of immense grief and trauma. These policies destroyed familial bonds and disrupted the transmission of cultural knowledge, leaving lasting scars on First Nations peoples.

The effects of the 'Stolen Generation' are still felt today. Intergenerational trauma manifests in higher rates of mental health issues, substance abuse, and socio-economic disadvantage amongst First Nations communities. The 'National Apology' delivered by Labor Prime Minister, Kevin Rudd, (Commonwealth of Australia 2008) was a significant step toward acknowledging this dark chapter in Australia's history, but the journey toward healing and reconciliation is ongoing.

Post-Colonial Policy and Recognition Efforts

Despite the significant harm caused by colonisation, there have been efforts to recognise and address the injustices faced by First Nations peoples. The 1967 Referendum marked a turning point, allowing Australia's First Nations peoples to be counted in the national census and granting the federal government the power to legislate on their behalf.

In 1992, the landmark Mabo Decision overturned the concept of 'terra nullius', recognising the traditional land rights of First Nations peoples. This led to the enactment of the Native Title Act, which provided a legal framework for First Nations communities to claim land rights.

The establishment of National Sorry Day and the ongoing work of the Reconciliation Movement and National

Aborigines and Islanders Day Observance Committee (NAIDOC) highlight Australia's commitment to addressing its colonial past. However, challenges remain, particularly in closing the gap between Indigenous and non-Indigenous Australians in health, education, and employment outcomes.

The Gold Rush Era and Diverse Influx (1850s)

The discovery of gold in the 1850s attracted a global influx of fortune seekers. While the majority hailed from Britain, Ireland, and Scotland, significant numbers arrived from China and Germany. Notably, Indian (Punjabi) hawkers and Punjabi / Afghan cameleers played crucial roles in establishing trade routes across Australia, facilitating commerce and cultural exchange (NLA 2024). Current research suggests that the majority of the Punjabi cameleers and hawkers were Sikhs (Wynne 2018).

The Immigration Restriction Act of 1901

On 23 December 1901, the newly formed Federal Parliament enacted the Immigration Restriction Act, aiming to limit non-British migration. Introduced by Protectionist (Liberal) Party Prime Minister, Edmund Barton, the legislation included a dictation test in any European language, effectively restricting non-European immigrants (NLA 2024).

Post-World War II Migration and Population Policies

The aftermath of World War II prompted Australia to reassess its population strategies. The bombing of Darwin in 1942 underscored the nation's vulnerability, leading to a push for population growth to bolster defence and development. In 1945, Labor MP Arthur Calwell was appointed as the first Minister for Immigration. He advocated for a substantial increase in population, stating, "If Australians have learned one lesson from the Pacific war... it is surely that we cannot continue to hold our island continent for ourselves and our descendants unless we greatly increase our numbers." (NLA 2024). This period saw the introduction of the "Ten-Pound Pom" scheme, offering assisted passage to British migrants, and the acceptance of displaced persons from various European countries.

Dismantling the 'White Australia Policy'

The 1950s and 1960s marked a gradual shift away from racially exclusive immigration policies. In 1957, the Menzies Liberal Government relaxed restrictions, allowing non-European migrants to obtain citizenship after 15 years of residency. The Migration Act 1958, amended by the Liberal Holt Government in 1966, further eased these restrictions. The final vestiges of the 'White Australia policy' were removed in 1973 by the Labor Government under Prime Minister Gough Whitlam (NLA 2024).

Humanitarian Intake and Refugee Resettlement

The 1970s and 1980s witnessed Australia opening its doors to refugees fleeing conflicts and political unrest. Significant groups included Lebanese and Cypriot refugees escaping civil wars, Vietnamese and Cambodian refugees from the Indochina conflicts, and East Timorese fleeing Indonesian occupation (NLA 2024). The Liberal Government, under Prime Minister Malcolm Fraser played a pivotal role in resettling these refugees, reflecting a commitment to humanitarian principles.

Evolution of Immigration Policy in the Late 20th Century

The late 20th century saw a shift in immigration focus towards skilled migration and family reunification. The 1990s experienced a rise in temporary migration, with policies adapting to global economic changes. However, the arrival of asylum seekers by boat, particularly from the Middle East and Sri Lanka, led to stringent measures, including offshore detention - a policy that has faced criticism from international human rights organisations (SBS 2013).

Contemporary Immigration Landscape

In recent decades, Australia has maintained a robust immigration program, with an annual intake of approximately 190,000 permanent migrants (SBS 2013). Temporary arrivals, including international students and skilled workers, who have also contributed significantly to population growth. The 2016 census revealed a diverse nation, with nearly half of all Australians born overseas or having at least one parent born abroad. The most common countries of birth after Australia were England, New Zealand, China, and India.

This historical overview underscores the dynamic nature of Australia's immigration policies and their profound impact on the nation's cultural fabric. Understanding this evolution is essential for shaping inclusive policies that reflect Australia's diverse society.

Conclusion: A Foundation for Cultural Education

The history of First Nations peoples in Australia is a story of resilience in the face of immense adversity. Their languages, traditions, and spiritual connections to the land are integral to Australia's identity and offer profound lessons about sustainability, community, and belonging.

By integrating First Nations perspectives into education and policy, Australia can begin to redress historical injustices and build a society that values diversity and inclusivity. Understanding this history is not just a scholarly pursuit - it is a moral imperative that underpins the broader framework of Cultural Education.

Chapter 3
The Role of Cultural Education in Shaping Policy

Cultural Education is not merely an academic exercise; it is a transformative framework that influences societal attitudes, bolsters social cohesion, and shapes inclusive policies. By cultivating awareness, sensitivity, and acceptance, Cultural Education empowers individuals and communities to bridge divides, promote mutual respect, and advocate towards unity within our diversity. This chapter explores the interplay between Cultural Education and policy formation, drawing from global examples, challenges, and successes, with a special emphasis on Bhutan's Gross National Happiness (GNH) framework and its profound implications for education and societal well-being.

The Interplay Between Cultural Education and Policy Formation

Education and policy are inextricably linked. Policies often reflect the collective values of a society, which are nurtured and shaped through education. Cultural Education plays a pivotal role in this process, creating informed citizens who can advocate for equitable and inclusive policies.

In Australia, this dynamic is exemplified by debates surrounding events like Australia Day, a day that evokes mixed emotions and perspectives. For First Nations peoples, it is a reminder of colonisation and dispossession but also a moment to reflect on resilience and contributions to the nation's identity. For other

Australians, it serves as a celebration of gratitude for the opportunities and prosperity this land offers. Balancing these perspectives requires Cultural Education that acknowledges historical injustices while promoting a shared vision for the future.

As Australia contemplates becoming a republic, the challenge lies in unifying these perspectives. A republic presents an opportunity to adopt a single flag that symbolises unity, moving away from the current division represented by the Australian, Aboriginal, and Torres Strait Islander flags flown side by side. While these flags hold deep significance, a shared national symbol could represent a commitment to a united future, one where all Australians feel equally acknowledged and valued.

Case Study: The Guru Nanak Lake Controversy

The naming of Berwick Springs Lake to 'Guru Nanak Lake' in South East Melbourne, Australia (November 2024), highlights the complexities of cultural representation in policy. The Victorian Labor Government intended the naming to honour the Sikh community for its immense contributions, particularly during crises like COVID-19, bushfires, and floods. Sikh Australians have consistently demonstrated their commitment to serving others, embodying the Australian values of mateship and mutual aid.

However, the process lacked adequate community consultation, which alienated sections of the broader population and fuelled backlash. The Liberal Party capitalised on this division, using the issue to stoke cultural tensions rather than enrich understanding. This incident underscores the importance of transparent and inclusive decision-making in policy formation. Recognising and celebrating cultural contributions must go hand-in-hand with engaging all stakeholders to build consensus rather than division (Hannaford 2024).

Policies reflect the prevailing attitudes and values within a society, and education plays a vital role in shaping these attitudes. Culturally aware citizens are more likely to advocate for inclusive policies, creating a positive feedback loop between education and governance. The relationship between Cultural Education and policy can be observed through case studies where public sentiment has driven legislative changes or where a lack of education has exacerbated social divides.

For example, in Australia, public awareness campaigns and school curricula addressing First Nations histories have influenced reconciliation efforts. The inclusion of Aboriginal and Torres Strait Islander perspectives in the national curriculum instils understanding and empathy from an early age, contributing to the momentum behind initiatives like the 'National Apology' to the 'Stolen Generation'. However, challenges persist, such as the lack of widespread understanding of Indigenous land rights, as evidenced by debates surrounding the Voice to Parliament referendum in 2023 called by Labor Prime Minister, Anthony Albanese.

In Australia, programs like Harmony Day celebrate cultural diversity and encourage communities to engage in intercultural dialogue. While such initiatives have been successful in building inclusivity, their impact is limited without systemic policy support. The naming of Guru Nanak Lake underscores the potential for grassroots movements to spark important conversations about cultural representation, even when outcomes remain contentious (Bureau Report 2024).

In the United States, grassroots advocacy has played a significant role in pushing for policies that address systemic racism and promote equity. For example, the Black Lives Matter movement has brought issues of racial justice to the forefront, influencing educational curricula to include African American history more prominently. However, these changes have faced resistance in certain states, highlighting the polarised nature of Cultural Education in the U.S. (Parker et al. 2020).

In Germany, grassroots organisations have worked to integrate refugees through Cultural Education programs, particularly in the wake of the 2015 migration crisis. These initiatives include language classes, cultural orientation workshops, and mentorship programs, which have helped mitigate social tensions and support refugee integration. However, far-right political movements have capitalised on fears surrounding immigration, demonstrating the ongoing need for systemic Cultural Education to counteract misinformation (Deutsche Welle 2019).

Global Perspectives on Cultural Education and Policy

Different countries provide valuable insights into how Cultural Education can shape societal attitudes and policies, with notable successes and failures offering lessons for Australia.

Bhutan: Integrating Happiness and Heritage

Bhutan's GNH framework embeds cultural preservation and mindfulness into education, nurturing a deep connection to heritage and well-being. Schools emphasise gratitude, respect, and environmental stewardship alongside academics, contributing to societal harmony and high happiness levels. While Bhutan excels in integrating cultural values into national development, its model highlights the balance required between tradition and modernisation (MOE 2014).

Japan: Values Before Academics

Japan prioritises values-based education in the early years, teaching children respect, gratitude, and community responsibility before introducing academic subjects. This approach has established societal harmony and high levels of mutual respect, even in an ethnically homogenous society. This 'cradle to grave' approach has far reaching appeal. However, Japan's struggle to integrate immigrant communities underscores the need for a more inclusive Cultural Education framework (MECSSTJ 2023).

Canada: Integrative Policies and Multiculturalism

Canada's multicultural policies have been highly effective in promoting inclusivity. From incorporating Indigenous studies into primary and secondary education to offering French immersion and Indigenous language programs, Canada actively upholds a sense of unity in diversity. According to a 2020 survey by the Environics Institute, 81% of Canadians view multiculturalism as a defining characteristic of their national identity. This proactive approach, including at the Political representation perspective, has strengthened social cohesion and immigrant integration while reinforcing Canada's global reputation as a leader in diversity (Environics Institute 2020).

England: The Pitfalls of Avoiding Difficult Conversations

England's approach to Cultural Education and integration has faced significant challenges, leading to increased polarisation and social fragmentation. Scholars have

47

identified several key issues contributing to these outcomes:

Inconsistent Integration of Diversity Education

The incorporation of diversity education into England's curricula has been sporadic and lacks a cohesive strategy. This inconsistency hampers the development of a comprehensive understanding of multiculturalism among students. As noted by the European Commission Against Racism and Intolerance (ECRI 2024), the absence of a standardised approach to diversity education results in varied experiences for students, depending on their school's commitment to these principles.

Political Reluctance to Address Islamophobia

Political hesitation to confront Islamophobia directly has exacerbated feelings of marginalisation within Muslim communities. The Aziz Foundation's report, "Institutionalised: The Rise of Islamophobia in Higher Education," highlights how anti-Muslim sentiments have become embedded within major institutions, including universities. This institutionalised Islamophobia not only alienates Muslim students and staff but also perpetuates negative stereotypes, hindering efforts toward genuine integration (Aziz 2024).

Rise of Nationalist Rhetoric

The lack of proactive Cultural Education and the failure to address biases have created a fertile ground for nationalist rhetoric. The resurgence of English nationalism, particularly in the context of events like Brexit, reflects deep-seated anxieties about national identity and cultural change. Scholars argue that this resurgence is partly due to the state's inability to reinforce a cohesive national identity that embraces diversity.

Erosion of Social Cohesion

The culmination of these factors has led to a significant erosion of social cohesion. The failure to implement robust Cultural Education policies and to confront societal biases has widened divisions, creating segregated communities and encouraging mutual distrust. This fragmentation poses a cautionary tale for other nations, underscoring the importance of comprehensive Cultural Education and proactive policies in maintaining social harmony.

Global Challenges and Opportunities

Examining the successes and failures of Cultural Education and immigration policies worldwide reveals critical insights:

Australia's approach to cultural diversity encompasses both commendable initiatives and areas requiring improvement. An examination of current legislation and practices reveals a complex landscape.

Positive Legislative Frameworks and Practices

1. **Anti-Discrimination Laws:** Australia has enacted comprehensive anti-discrimination legislation, including the Racial Discrimination Act 1975, which prohibits discrimination based on race, colour, descent, national or ethnic origin. This legal framework establishes a foundation for protecting individuals from racial discrimination.

2. **Multicultural Policies:** The Australian government has implemented policies promoting multiculturalism, recognising the cultural diversity of its population. These policies aim to elicit social cohesion and inclusivity by encouraging the celebration of diverse cultures.

3. **Educational Initiatives:** Programs have been introduced to incorporate Cultural Education into school curricula, aiming to enhance students' understanding and appreciation of different cultures (ACARA 2023). These initiatives seek to build a more inclusive society by educating the younger generation about cultural diversity.

Challenges and Areas for Improvement

1. **Inconsistent Implementation of Multicultural Policies:** Despite the existence of multicultural policies, their application across different states and territories is inconsistent. This inconsistency can lead to disparities in how cultural diversity is managed and celebrated nationwide.

2. **Rising Nationalist Sentiments:** Australia has experienced an increase in nationalist rhetoric, which poses challenges to social cohesion. This trend underscores the need for continuous efforts to promote inclusivity and counter divisive narratives.

3. **First Nations Rights and Recognition:** While there have been steps toward recognising First Nations Australians, such as the establishment of the Voice to Parliament in South Australia, there is ongoing debate and criticism regarding the adequacy of these measures. Advocates argue for

more substantial reforms to address historical injustices and ensure meaningful representation.

4. **Treatment of Migrants and Refugees:** Recent legislative proposals have raised concerns among human rights groups. For instance, bills introduced by the Albanese Government have been criticised for potentially undermining the rights of migrants and refugees, suggesting a need for policies that balance national security with humanitarian obligations (Yallop and Yosufzai 2024).

Successes:

- **Canada**: Policies that integrate multicultural education into all levels of schooling have solidified a strong sense of national unity while respecting diversity (Porter 2004).

- **New Zealand**: The incorporation of Māori language and culture into the national curriculum has contributed to a resurgence of pride in Indigenous heritage among both Māori and non-Māori citizens (NZME 2023).

Failures:

- **England**: Despite efforts to promote multiculturalism, policies have failed to address underlying biases, racially motivated violence, leading to increased Islamophobia and community fragmentation (ECARI 2024).

- **France**: The strict secularism enforced in schools has often marginalised religious minorities, particularly Muslim students, who feel their identities are not respected (ECARI 2021).

Opportunities:
- **Australia**: Expanding cross-curriculum priorities to include deeper engagement with migrant histories could enhance cultural understanding.

- **Global Collaborations**: Sharing best practices across countries, such as Canada's language immersion programs or Germany's refugee integration initiatives, could inform more effective policies.

The Power of Representation

When diverse cultures are represented in education, politics and media, inclusivity becomes normalised, breaking down barriers of "otherness" and creating a sense of belonging. Education systems around the world demonstrate varying degrees of success in incorporating cultural representation into curricula.

In Sweden, the integration of democratic values and respect for cultural diversity into early childhood education has contributed to high levels of social trust. However, challenges remain in addressing the needs of immigrant communities, particularly regarding language acquisition and socio-economic inclusion. The Swedish school system offers "Swedish as a Second Language" programs, yet gaps in outcomes for non-native speakers persist, illustrating the need for holistic support beyond the classroom (SNAE 2023).

Bhutan: Lessons for Cultural Education

Bhutan's GNH framework offers a unique perspective on how Cultural Education can influence societal well-being and policy formation.

1. **Cultural Preservation and Education:** Bhutan's focus on cultural preservation instils a

sense of pride and identity in its citizens. Schools teach traditional songs, dances, and crafts, ensuring that students grow up with a strong connection to their heritage.

2. **Measuring Happiness Through Education:** The GNH index evaluates societal progress through factors like psychological well-being and cultural diversity. This holistic approach provides a compelling model for integrating Cultural Education into national development strategies (OECD 2024).

3. **Policy Implications:** Bhutan's policies prioritise cultural and environmental sustainability over material wealth. This alignment of education and governance creates a society that values well-being and equity over economic growth alone.

4. **Economic Development and Technological Advancement:** Bhutan has embraced technological progress to enhance economic growth while upholding its cultural values. Initiatives like the "Digital Bhutan" strategy aim to increase the digital economy's GDP contribution to 10% by 2034 and create 1,000 jobs annually starting in 2024 (being mindful that Bhutan's population in 2023 is 787,424, whilst Australia's is 26million). The Government is investing in digital infrastructure, including National Digital Identity and digital payment systems, to facilitate this transformation (GovTech 2024).
Additionally, Bhutan is focusing on renewable energy, leveraging its hydro, solar, and wind resources to promote sustainable development and consciously driving its carbon footprint down.

5. **Cultural Homogeneity and Its Impact:** Bhutan's relatively monocultural society has enabled a unified approach to implementing the GNH framework. The emphasis on a singular

cultural identity has facilitated cohesive policy-making and societal acceptance of GNH principles. However, this homogeneity also presents challenges, particularly in accommodating diverse perspectives and integrating minority groups. The government's focus on cultural preservation sometimes leads to tensions between maintaining tradition and embracing modernity (OECD 2024).

Challenges and Opportunities in Australia

Australia faces unique challenges in integrating Cultural Education into policy formation but also has significant opportunities to lead by example.

Challenges

- **Polarised Narratives:** Debates around Australia Day and immigration policies highlight deep divisions that Cultural Education must address.
- **Representation Gaps:** First Nations and migrant histories are underrepresented in many curricula, limiting students' understanding of the nation's diversity.
- **Structural Barriers:** Economic and social inequalities continue to hinder the inclusion of marginalised communities.

Opportunities

1. **Expanding the Curriculum:** Building on cross-curriculum priorities, Australian schools can incorporate global citizenship education and lessons on the contributions of diverse communities. Australia can adopt a more inclusive curriculum by integrating stories of migrant contributions alongside First Nations histories. This would create a richer understanding of the nation's diverse heritage.

2. **Promoting Cultural Literacy in Businesses:**
   Workplace training programs can reduce discrimination, improve collaboration, and enhance innovation, creating a ripple effect across society. Drawing inspiration from Japan's early focus on values, Australian schools could introduce programs that emphasise empathy, gratitude, and community responsibility from a young age. These lessons could be built upon in secondary education with global citizenship and intercultural communication training.
3. **Engaging Communities:** Initiatives like Harmony Day can be expanded to include year-round programs that celebrate cultural diversity and facilitate dialogues between communities.
4. **Learning from Bhutan and Japan:** Australia can adapt Bhutan's holistic approach to cultural preservation and Japan's emphasis on values education, and strong economic progress thrust to strengthen social cohesion and mutual respect.
5. **Supporting Businesses in Cultural Competency:**
   Workplace Cultural Education programs can improve collaboration, reduce discrimination, and enhance innovation. Incentives for businesses to implement such programs could drive widespread adoption.
6. **National Consultation on Unity Symbols:**
   If Australia moves toward becoming a republic, a national conversation about adopting a new flag and unifying cultural symbols could serve as a catalyst for collective identity building.

Actions for Positive Outcomes

To realise the potential of Cultural Education in shaping policy, Australia must take concrete steps:

1. **Government Commitment:**
   - Establish a national framework for Cultural Education that integrates First Nations, migrant, and global perspectives.
   - Increase funding for cultural programs in schools and communities.
2. **Educational Reform:**
   - Standardise the teaching of First Nations histories and migrant contributions across all states and territories.
   - Introduce values-based education in early childhood to cultivate empathy and community responsibility.
   - Provide more teacher resources on Cultural Education by encouraging diverse authors and artists to create Australian specific books and resources that represent all Australians.
3. **Policy Development:**
   - Align immigration and multicultural policies with Cultural Education initiatives to promote inclusivity.
   - Use Bhutan's GNH framework as inspiration for measuring societal well-being beyond economic indicators.
4. **Corporate Collaboration:**
   - Encourage businesses to adopt diversity and inclusion training, tying these practices to measurable outcomes like employee satisfaction and productivity.
   - Create unified approach to Cultural Workplace Reviews.
   - Creating a DEI policy is not enough, it needs to be implemented and reflected across all levels of organisations.

Conclusion: A Framework for Policy Formation and Unified Vision for the Future

Cultural Education is a transformative force, laying the foundation for inclusive policies and societal cohesion. By examining global successes and challenges, it is evident that effective frameworks must balance representation, grassroots advocacy, and systemic policy support. From Bhutan's GNH index prioritising cultural preservation to Canada's comprehensive multicultural policies and Japan's values-based education, these examples offer pathways to embed Cultural Education in governance and daily life.

Australia stands at a crossroads, with a legislative framework that champions diversity but faces challenges in implementation, nationalism, and the treatment of First Nations and migrant communities. Addressing these gaps requires a holistic approach: recognising biases, supporting open dialogue, and aligning actions with the nation's multicultural ideals. Lessons from around the globe show that systemic Cultural Education can unite communities, empower individuals, and strengthen societal well-being.

Cultural Education is not merely an academic exercise - it is a call to action for policymakers, educators, corporations, and citizens to commit to inclusion and equity. By embracing sensitivity, awareness, and responsiveness, Australia can pave the way for a future where diversity is not just accepted but celebrated, ensuring that every citizen feels valued, empowered, and united under a shared vision for progress.

Chapter 4
Cultural Change as a Driver for Corporate Success

Cultural diversity and inclusion are not just moral imperatives; they are strategic advantages that can significantly enhance business performance. Companies that embrace Cultural Education and nurture inclusive environments reap benefits ranging from increased innovation and market expansion to improved employee satisfaction and financial success. In contrast, organisations that fail to prioritise diversity and inclusion often face reputational, operational, and financial risks. This chapter explores the business case for Cultural Education, illustrating its critical role in driving corporate success.

The Business Case for Inclusion

1. Innovation Through Diversity

Diverse teams bring together varied perspectives, experiences, and problem-solving approaches, which are critical for stimulating innovation. A study by McKinsey & Company found that companies in the top quartile for ethnic and racial diversity were 36% more likely to outperform their peers in profitability (Hunt et al. 2020).

For example, Google's commitment to diversity has been instrumental in its innovative culture. By establishing an environment where diverse ideas are welcomed, Google has developed products that resonate globally, from multilingual search capabilities to culturally sensitive marketing campaigns. This success stems from its investment in employee resource groups, unconscious bias training, and DEI programs (GDR 2023).

2. Market Expansion

Understanding diverse markets allows companies to tailor products and services to meet the needs of a broader customer base. The Commonwealth Bank of Australia (CBA) is a prime example of this strategy. Recognising the multicultural makeup of Australia, the bank offers culturally sensitive financial products, multilingual customer service, and support for culturally significant events.

CBA's initiatives have not only strengthened customer loyalty but also positioned the bank as a leader in the financial services sector. Its inclusive policies demonstrate that Cultural Education is not just about internal equity but also about external engagement and market relevance (CBA 2023).

The Triple Bottom Line: People, Planet, Profit

1. People: Enhancing Employee Engagement and Satisfaction

Investing in Cultural Education creates psychologically safe workplaces where employees feel valued and respected. This psychological safety, a concept popularised by Harvard researcher Amy Edmondson, is linked to higher employee engagement and productivity (Edmondson 2024).

In Australia, Telstra has implemented Cultural Education programs to support its diverse workforce. These initiatives have resulted in increased employee satisfaction and reduced staff turnover, demonstrating that inclusivity is integral to talent retention and organisational success (Telstra 2023).

2. Planet: Aligning with Sustainability Goals

Cultural Education also intersects with environmental sustainability, as organisations learn to engage with communities in ways that respect local traditions and values. For instance, multinational corporations operating in the lands of the First Nations peoples, such as mining companies in Australia, are increasingly adopting culturally informed practices to minimise environmental and social impacts.

3. Profit: Boosting Financial Performance

A study by Deloitte (2021) revealed that inclusive companies are twice as likely to meet or exceed financial targets. The alignment of people and planet with profit underscores the importance of a holistic approach to corporate strategy.

When Diversity Initiatives Miss the Mark

The consequences of cultural insensitivity or poorly executed diversity initiatives can ripple through an organisation, undermining morale and trust. A recent experience highlights the dangers of mishandled Cultural Education in the workplace.

While working with a Melbourne-based organisation on implementing DEI initiatives, I observed a situation where good intentions went awry. As part of their Reconciliation Action Plan (RAP), the organisation invited a representative from the local First Nations community to deliver a cultural practices workshop. While this initiative aimed to promote understanding and reconciliation, the session ended up leaving the staff feeling deflated, demotivated, angry, and upset.

The elder sent to conduct the workshop was a victim of the 'stolen generation'. He adopted a highly confrontational approach, placing blame squarely on "white people" for historical and ongoing injustices. The tone of the session was relentlessly critical, to the point of telling staff members that there was no point in pursuing a RAP because it was merely a tokenistic gesture and that the organisation did not truly care about First Nations peoples.

This approach, rather than encouraging dialogue, trust, and collaboration, created resentment and a sense of futility among the staff. While the anger and frustration expressed by the elder were valid reflections of lived experiences, the lack of alignment with the session's purpose - building understanding and cooperation - led to counterproductive outcomes.

1. Public Relations Crises

Cultural insensitivity can have far-reaching consequences for businesses, damaging their reputations, alienating customers, and causing financial losses. A prime example is the 2019 controversy involving luxury fashion brand Gucci, which released a sweater that bore an uncanny resemblance to blackface, a deeply offensive and historically charged symbol of racism. The sweater, part of Gucci's winter collection, featured a high black turtleneck with oversized red lips that evoked painful imagery tied to minstrel shows in the United States and elsewhere.

The backlash was immediate and widespread, with public figures, celebrities, and social justice advocates condemning the brand for its apparent ignorance. Social media amplified the outrage, leading to calls for boycotts and sparking debates about corporate responsibility and the need for diversity in decision-making. Critics pointed out that the sweater's design likely passed through multiple layers of approval without anyone recognising its offensive nature, highlighting a glaring lack of cultural awareness within the organisation.

In response, Gucci issued public apologies, removed the product from its stores, and initiated damage-control measures, including mandatory cultural sensitivity training for employees and the formation of a global diversity and inclusion council. Gucci's CEO, Marco Bizzarri, acknowledged the brand's failure to reflect its values of inclusivity and diversity and committed to long-term changes, including hiring more diverse talent to prevent similar incidents in the future (Hsu and Paton 2019).

This incident serves as a powerful example of how companies can unintentionally perpetuate harmful stereotypes when they fail to prioritise Cultural Education and inclusivity at every level of their operations. In a globalised and socially conscious marketplace, brands are expected to understand and respect cultural nuances. Oversights like Gucci's not only harm the affected communities but also risk alienating loyal customers, tarnishing brand equity, and reducing shareholder confidence.

To avoid such crises, businesses must embed cultural awareness into their corporate DNA, ensuring that diversity and inclusion are not merely afterthoughts but integral to decision-making processes. This includes involving diverse voices in product design, marketing strategies, and leadership roles to better reflect and respect the global audience they serve.

2. Employee Morale and Retention
Workplaces that fail to implement inclusivity risk not only their external reputation but also their internal cohesion and productivity. Research by the Society for

Human Resource Management found that 25% of employees leave their jobs due to a lack of inclusion, a significant factor contributing to workplace dissatisfaction and disengagement (SHRM 2020). High turnover rates are costly, both financially and culturally, as organisations lose valuable institutional knowledge and disrupt team dynamics.

One critical yet often overlooked aspect of inclusivity in the workplace is the role of language, which begins at the recruitment stage. The language used in job advertisements, interview processes, and internal communications can profoundly influence how potential and current employees perceive an organisation. For instance, recruitment advertisements should use language that appeals to a diverse talent pool by avoiding jargon, culturally exclusive terms, or overly aggressive phrasing, which can deter candidates from underrepresented groups. Instead of framing application outcomes negatively, such as using the word "rejected," organisations can adopt more empathetic and inclusive terminology like "not selected." This small yet impactful change reflects a culture of understanding and respect, which helps create a psychologically safe environment for candidates and employees alike.

Moreover, the lack of cultural sensitivity in workplace communications or policies can lead to feelings of exclusion amongst employees from diverse backgrounds. Employees who perceive their workplaces as non-inclusive often report feeling undervalued, misunderstood, or even marginalised. This lack of empathy can result in disengagement, reduced morale, and an erosion of trust between employees and management. Ultimately, such environments contribute to attrition, with employees seeking workplaces where they feel seen, heard, and respected.

Inclusive language and cultural awareness extend beyond recruitment into everyday workplace interactions. A simple gesture, such as learning to pronounce an employee's name correctly or providing a platform for underrepresented voices during meetings, can significantly impact morale. These actions signal that diversity is not just a checkbox for compliance but a deeply embedded organisational value.

Inclusive workplaces also experience higher employee retention and satisfaction. When employees feel a sense of belonging and alignment with their organisation's values, they are more likely to contribute meaningfully to their roles, collaborate effectively with colleagues, and remain loyal to their employer. Empathy plays a crucial role in this equation, enabling managers and teams to address misunderstandings, resolve conflicts, and build cohesive working relationships.

By prioritising Cultural Education and embedding inclusivity into their organisational practices, businesses can unlock the full potential of their workforce. This involves not only recruiting diverse talent but also sustaining an environment where everyone, regardless of their background, feels supported, motivated, and empowered to thrive. Ultimately, such investments in inclusivity yield long-term benefits: increased innovation, stronger team cohesion, and enhanced organisational resilience.

Case Studies: The Correlation Between Inclusion and Success

Global Comparisons: Lessons from Around the World

- **Norway**: Norway mandates gender diversity on corporate boards, with women required to hold at least 40% of board seats. This policy has enhanced governance and decision-making, proving the economic advantages of inclusivity (Catalyst 2021).

- **South Africa**: Post-apartheid policies, such as Black Economic Empowerment (BEE), have aimed to address historical inequalities. While these initiatives have faced challenges, they underscore the importance of integrating social justice into corporate strategy (Acemoglu et al. 2007).

Breaking Barriers: Addressing the Glass Ceiling

The glass ceiling - a metaphor for the invisible barriers preventing marginalised groups from advancing - remains a significant issue (Wilson 2014). Women, people of colour, and individuals from Culturally and Linguistically Diverse (CALD) backgrounds often face systemic biases that hinder career progression.

1. Gender Disparities

While women are breaking barriers in many industries, they remain underrepresented in leadership roles. In Australia, women hold only 19.4% of CEO positions in ASX200 companies, despite making up nearly half the workforce (WGEA 2023).

2. Racial and Ethnic Inequalities

People of colour face additional hurdles due to unconscious biases and systemic discrimination. Research by the Diversity Council of Australia found that individuals from CALD backgrounds are 30% less likely to be promoted compared to their non-CALD counterparts (DCA 2022). Australia also faces a real threat of "reverse migration" which is expanded in Chapter 6.

The Case for Leadership Diversity and Equity in Australian Corporations

Diversity in senior leadership is often touted as a cornerstone of inclusion, but practical implementation remains inconsistent. A study of the CBA underscores this disparity, particularly concerning ethnic diversity in executive roles. Despite its commitment to gender equity and accessibility, CBA's leadership team remains predominantly Anglo-Saxon, highlighting the gap between policy aspirations and on-ground realities (CBA 2023).

Drawing from *Equity Theory* and *Stereotype Threat* (Northouse 2018), this case study explores the psychological and systemic barriers to representation in leadership. The absence of visible role models from diverse ethnic backgrounds may contribute to perceptions of inequity and negatively impact employee motivation and performance. Furthermore, stereotype threats - exacerbated by underrepresentation - can hinder the advancement of talented employees from minority groups.

Analytical frameworks such as *gap analysis* and *benchmarking* (Kemmerer and Arnold 1993) reveal critical misalignments between corporate goals and outcomes. Benchmarking against industry standards and implementing targeted measures could allow institutions like CBA to bridge these gaps, promoting not only equity but also innovation and improved performance metrics.

This analysis serves as a microcosm for broader trends in Australian corporate culture. While strides have been made in gender inclusion, ethnic diversity (especially in senior leadership roles) lags, underscoring the need for actionable, data-driven strategies that go beyond symbolic commitments. Incorporating these learnings into Cultural Education frameworks ensures future leaders understand and address such disparities, aligning corporate practices with Australia's multicultural ethos.

Leadership, Motivation, and Organisational Effectiveness in Cultural Education

Leadership and motivation play a pivotal role in fostering cultural understanding, inclusivity, and societal cohesion. Whether in educational institutions, workplaces, or community settings, effective leadership is essential for creating environments where diversity is celebrated, and individuals are empowered to reach their potential. The interplay between leadership, motivation, and organisational effectiveness is deeply influenced by how well systems align incentives with long-term cultural goals.

Aligning Incentives with Cultural Goals

Organisational and educational structures often falter when incentives do not align with desired outcomes. *On the Folly of Rewarding A, While Hoping for B* (Kerr 1975), highlights, that institutions frequently reward behaviours that conflict with their stated goals. For example, organisations may espouse values of collaboration, empathy, and inclusivity while incentivising individual achievements or short-term results (KPI's).

In the context of Cultural Education, this misalignment can have profound consequences. If educators or corporate leaders are rewarded solely based on performance metrics, such as test scores or quarterly profits, the broader goals of encouraging empathy, inclusivity, and cultural awareness may be neglected. This undermines efforts to create environments where cultural responsiveness is a priority.

In contrast, systems that align rewards with long-term goals - such as supporting diverse leadership, promoting team collaboration, or achieving societal cohesion - are better equipped to drive meaningful change. For example, organisations that integrate **team-based incentives** and **cultural competency training** into performance reviews often see higher engagement and alignment with their values.

Leadership in Driving Cultural Change
Leadership is not only about individual traits but also about creating and sustaining environments that empower others. Within the framework of Cultural Education, leaders have a unique responsibility to model inclusive behaviours and champion diversity. This role requires more than managerial skills; it demands a deep understanding of the social, cultural, and historical contexts that shape interactions in diverse settings.

The debate over whether leaders are "born or made" is particularly relevant here. While research indicates that approximately 30% of leadership traits may be heritable, the remaining 70% are shaped by environmental factors such as education, mentorship, and lived experiences (Avolio and Hannah 2020). This suggests that leadership potential exists in many individuals and can be nurtured through intentional efforts (Boerma et al. 2017).

For example, effective leadership in Cultural Education programs often involves mentorship models where experienced leaders guide younger or less experienced individuals from underrepresented. By doing so, they not only transfer skills but also provide role models that challenge stereotypes and broaden perspectives.

Case Study: Leadership as a Catalyst for Inclusivity

A notable example of leadership driving cultural inclusivity is the approach taken by educational institutions that prioritise diverse representation in leadership roles. For instance, schools that actively recruit leaders from varied cultural and linguistic backgrounds create a trickle-down effect, empowering students from those communities to see themselves represented and valued. Similarly, corporations that prioritise promoting women and minorities into leadership roles often report higher levels of employee satisfaction, innovation, and societal impact.

Motivation and the Role of Cultural Education

Cultural Education is intrinsically linked to motivation, both at an individual and organisational level. Vroom's Expectancy Theory (1964) highlights that individuals are motivated when they perceive a clear connection between their efforts, the outcomes they desire, and the rewards they receive. This theory is particularly relevant in the context of Cultural Education, where the "reward" often takes the form of a more inclusive, equitable, and cohesive society.

For example, students and employees who understand the broader impact of their actions - such as reducing biases, cultivating belonging, or breaking down barriers - are more likely to engage meaningfully with Cultural Education initiatives. However, if the connection between their efforts and the outcomes is unclear or poorly communicated, motivation may falter.

By aligning educational policies, workplace incentives, and leadership development programs with the broader goals of cultural responsiveness, societies can create a virtuous cycle where motivated individuals drive systemic change, and systemic change, in turn, reinforces individual motivation.

Organisational Ambidexterity

Organisational ambidexterity, or the ability to balance exploration and exploitation, is another critical component of effective leadership. Companies that can innovate while refining existing practices are better positioned to adapt to changing environments (Umans et al. 2018). For instance, aligning incentives with long-term objectives, such as nurturing Cultural Education within workplaces, can yield both immediate and sustainable benefits.

In one not-for-profit organisation I worked with, innovation in digital education platforms was seamlessly integrated with traditional cultural content, achieving both disruption and continuity. This approach, enabled by clear leadership and aligned incentives, exemplifies the power of ambidexterity in achieving organisational and societal goals.

Actionable Steps for Businesses

To harness the benefits of Cultural Education, businesses must adopt strategic approaches:

1. **Integrate Cultural Education into Training Programs**:
   Develop comprehensive programs that address unconscious biases, cultural competency, and inclusive leadership.
2. **Adopt Transparent DEI Policies**:
   Ensure that diversity and inclusion goals are measurable and tied to performance reviews.
3. **Prioritise Psychological Safety**:
   Create environments where employees feel safe to

express ideas, ask questions, and challenge the status quo without fear of retaliation.

4. **Engage in Community Partnerships**: Collaborate with local cultural organisations to build trust and demonstrate a commitment to inclusivity. Encourage staff to participate in volunteering. My sister's company incorporates four volunteer days a year, with the only requirement being to share the experience on internal communications platform.

5. **Track and Report Progress**: Use metrics to evaluate the impact of Cultural Education on employee satisfaction, retention, and financial performance.

Conclusion: The Path to Becoming an Employer of Choice

Cultural Education is not a box-ticking exercise; it is a strategic necessity that drives innovation, enhances employee engagement, and strengthens market positioning. By embracing inclusivity, companies can expand their talent pools, facilitate psychological safety, and achieve the triple bottom line of people, planet, and profit.

Organisations that prioritise Cultural Education and diversity will not only thrive in a competitive market but also set the standard for ethical and sustainable business practices. This approach ensures that businesses are not just workplaces but also catalysts for societal progress, paving the way for a more inclusive and prosperous future.

Chapter 5
From Bias to Belonging - The Power of Early Education

Addressing biases from an early age is one of the most effective ways to cultivate an inclusive society. Stereotypes and prejudices are not innate; they are learned behaviours influenced by family, media, educational environments, and societal structures. Early education has the unique ability to shape a child's worldview, making it a critical arena for interventions aimed at reducing bias and promoting cultural awareness. This chapter explores how biases form, the role of early education in counteracting them, and the measurable impact of such interventions.

Formation of Stereotypes and Biases

Stereotypes and biases begin forming at a remarkably young age. Research shows that by the age of three, children can absorb social cues, including those related to race, gender, and cultural differences. By age five, children often exhibit preferences or prejudices based on these cues (Mandalaywala et al. 2020).

1. Family and Social Circles
Children's first exposure to societal norms often comes from their immediate environment - families, caregivers, and social circles. Parental attitudes toward race, ethnicity, and culture heavily influence a child's perception of the world. A study published by the American Psychological Association found that children whose parents openly discussed diversity and inclusion

were more likely to exhibit empathy and tolerance (APA 2010).

However, families can also unintentionally pass down biases. Subtle comments, passing remarks, body language, a lack of diverse social interactions, or adherence to stereotypes reinforce prejudices that can become deeply ingrained. For instance, studies in the UK showed that children in homogenous communities were less likely to form inclusive attitudes compared to those in multicultural urban areas (BBC 2021).

2. Educational Materials

Textbooks, storybooks, and classroom discussions play a significant role in shaping children's perceptions. When educational content predominantly represents one culture or perspective, it reinforces the idea that other cultures are less valuable. A 2019 analysis of Australian school textbooks revealed a lack of representation of First Nations peoples and diverse migrant communities, perpetuating a Eurocentric narrative (ACARA 2023).

Conversely, inclusive educational materials can challenge stereotypes and broaden worldviews. Programs like *The World Is Our Playground* book series (Singh 2024), exemplify how diverse storytelling can help children appreciate different cultures by showcasing traditions, food, language, and shared humanity. These books are not only engaging stories but also valuable tools in promoting Cultural Education and inclusivity, addressing important issues to help promote awareness and acceptance while combatting racism and bullying. Minister for Immigration and Citizenship, Brendan O'Connor, highlighted the significance of inclusiveness, respect, and belonging in Australia's multicultural framework - values that resonate strongly with the themes of this series.

The series does more than entertain. It empowers students by ensuring they see themselves and their peers reflected in the books they read. When children of diverse backgrounds see characters who share their cultural heritage, traditions, or physical appearance in stories, it validates their identity and instils a sense of pride. These stories normalise a classroom where children from varied ethnicities, faiths, and traditions identify as Australian and are portrayed not in isolation but as part of a vibrant, collaborative community. By showcasing diverse characters working, playing, eating, dancing, and competing together in sport, the series nurtures an understanding that diversity is an integral part of being Australian.

The accompanying 'Parent/Teacher Resource Notes on Cultural Awareness' included in each book further amplify the series' educational value. These resources provide targeted vocabulary, structured activities, and discussion points to help educators unpack the cultural themes within the stories, creating opportunities to explore topics like inclusion, respect, and the shared values that unite us as Australians. The books, aimed at the Prep–2 reading level, align with Australia's national curriculum, ensuring young learners are exposed to lessons of unity within diversity during their formative years.

Initiatives like *The World is Our Playground* not only complement government efforts to build a diverse and inclusive educational environment but also play a crucial role in promoting social cohesion through education. By encouraging children to see themselves as part of a multicultural society, these stories build pride in the Australian identity - one defined by its rich cultural tapestry. The series underscores that understanding and respecting others' ethnicity is a cornerstone of social cohesion, paving the way for a more inclusive future.

The Role of Faith-Based Schools: Opportunities and Challenges

Faith-based schools, including Muslim, Jewish, and Christian institutions, play a significant role in Australia's educational landscape. These schools often excel in creating environments that promote strong community ties, moral guidance, and values-based learning. For many families, these institutions provide a sense of cultural and spiritual continuity, reinforcing their faith traditions and community identity. Such environments can offer a source of belonging, resilience, and moral grounding for students, equipping them with the ethical frameworks and self-belief often missing in secular education.

However, the presence of faith-based schools also raises challenges, particularly regarding inclusivity and societal integration. While these schools may form a deep connection to specific cultural or religious identities, they can inadvertently create silos, limiting students' exposure to diverse perspectives and lived experiences. This isolation risks reinforcing stereotypes or biases about other communities, which can hinder the development of broader social cohesion and cultural empathy.

Additionally, some faith-based schools have faced criticism for prioritising dogma over critical thinking, potentially limiting students' ability to engage with the plurality of beliefs and values present in contemporary Australian society. Instances where faith-based curricula omit or challenge mainstream scientific, historical, or social perspectives can further isolate students from the realities of a multicultural, secular democracy.

Furthermore, the selective nature of faith-based schools can lead to exclusionary practices, whether intentionally or unintentionally. In some cases, families from minority faiths or secular backgrounds may feel unwelcome or underrepresented within these institutions. For example, LGBTQ+ students or students from interfaith families may face additional barriers to acceptance, which can impact their mental health and sense of belonging.

To address these concerns, faith-based schools must embrace a dual responsibility: maintaining their cultural and religious ethos while cultivating inclusivity and cross-cultural understanding. Incorporating Cultural Education within faith-based curricula can bridge the gap between insular faith teachings and broader societal values which many are already doing. For instance:

- Encouraging interfaith dialogues and programs that expose students to diverse beliefs and practices.
- Embedding universal principles such as respect, empathy, and social justice within their teaching frameworks.
- Providing professional development for educators to ensure they are culturally responsive and equipped to support diverse student populations.

Faith-based schools, when aligned with the principles of inclusivity and mutual respect, have the potential to contribute meaningfully to Australia's social fabric. By promoting shared values alongside their religious teachings, these institutions can prepare students to thrive in a multicultural society while remaining grounded in their faith traditions. Addressing these dual objectives ensures that faith-based schools are not only places of learning but also agents of societal cohesion.

Early Intervention Strategies

Early education offers a powerful platform to challenge biases and cultivate inclusivity. Proactive strategies can transform the classroom into a space where diversity is celebrated and all children feel a sense of belonging.

1. Inclusive Curriculum

An inclusive curriculum incorporates stories, histories, and perspectives from a variety of cultures and communities.

- **Australia**
  In Australian classrooms, the gradual integration of First Nations histories and cultures under the Cross-Curriculum Priorities has been a step forward. However, inconsistencies in implementation highlight the need for stronger national overview and teacher training (ACARA 2023).

2. Interactive Learning

Interactive programs engage children in exploring diversity through hands-on activities. This also must include assisting children in discovering their own ethnicity and being empowered by it.

3. Parent-Teacher Collaboration

Educators and parents must work together to reinforce inclusive values. Parent workshops, diverse classroom events, and cultural exchange programs can help bridge the gap between school and home, creating a consistent message of acceptance.

The Correlation Between Bias and Mental Health

Unchecked biases and stereotypes not only harm marginalised communities but also negatively impact the mental health of all children.

- **The Impact of Exclusion**
  Studies show that children who experience racial or cultural exclusion are more likely to suffer from anxiety, depression, and low self-esteem (JAH 2020). For instance, First Nations children in Australia face higher rates of psychological distress due to systemic racism and historical trauma (Beyond Blue 2021).
- **Internalised Bias**
  Children from dominant cultural groups can develop guilt, fear, or anxiety when exposed to biased narratives. This internalised bias can hinder their ability to form genuine connections with peers from different backgrounds.
- **Resilience Through Education**
  Early interventions that promote diversity and inclusion can counteract these effects. Programs emphasising cultural pride, empathy, and mutual respect contribute to healthier self-esteem and interpersonal relationships.

Bullying and its correlation to Cultural Education

Bullying, particularly when rooted in racism, stereotypes, and cultural misunderstandings, has profound implications for mental health. Research indicates that ethno-cultural bullying - a form of interpersonal violence with discriminatory, racist, and/or xenophobic elements - can lead to significant psychological distress amongst victims (Rodriguez-Hidalgo et al. 2019).

Studies have shown that children and adolescents who experience racial or ethnic bullying are at an increased risk of developing mental health issues such as depression, anxiety, and low self-esteem. The internalisation of negative stereotypes and the stress associated with discrimination can exacerbate these conditions, leading to long-term psychological effects (Sapouna et al. 2023).

Moreover, the presence of biases and stereotypes in educational settings can contribute to a hostile environment, further perpetuating bullying behaviours. For instance, stereotypes can instigate aggression and peer conflicts among students of different racial and ethnic backgrounds, leading to exclusion and victimisation.

Addressing these issues requires comprehensive Cultural Education that promotes understanding and respect for diversity. By integrating cultural responsiveness into curricula and fostering inclusive environments, educators can mitigate the factors that contribute to bullying and its associated mental health impacts (MDPI 2022).

In summary, there is a clear correlation between bullying and factors such as racism, stereotypes, and cultural misunderstandings. Implementing effective Cultural Education and promoting inclusivity are essential steps in reducing bullying and supporting the mental health of all students.

Reflections on the Ripponlea Synagogue Attack

On the 6th December 2024 there was a firebombing of the Ripponlea Synagogue, now classified as a 'likely terrorist attack', is a stark reminder of the enduring presence of hate and intolerance in society. Acts of violence rooted in anti-Semitism strike at the heart of Australia's multicultural identity, shaking the foundations of social cohesion and community trust. While the government's swift condemnation and pledge for increased vigilance and funding for security are commendable, such reactions must transcend mere crisis management. To prevent future tragedies, Australia must invest in long-term, systemic solutions, starting with cultural education.

The incident underscores a critical gap in understanding and mutual respect amongst communities. Hate does not emerge in isolation; it is cultivated in environments of ignorance, fear, and bias. Cultural Education, implemented effectively from early childhood through adulthood, can play a transformative role in addressing these underlying issues. By equipping individuals with knowledge about diverse faiths, histories, and shared human values, Cultural Education develops empathy and dispels stereotypes that fuel hatred.

The Role of Policy and Social Cohesion Initiatives

The Australian government's response to this attack must include more than funding for security measures. While immediate safety is paramount, the long-term solution lies in building a society where such measures are less necessary. This can be achieved by:

1. **Integrating Holocaust and Religious Education:** Expanding curricula to include education about Jewish history, the Holocaust, and contributions of Jewish Australians. Such education not only honours the Jewish community but also raises awareness about the consequences of hatred and discrimination.

2. **Promoting Interfaith Dialogues:** Encouraging programs that bring together communities of different faiths, such as the Jewish, Christian, Muslim, and other communities, to share traditions, celebrate diversity, and find common ground.
3. **Community Empowerment:** Providing resources to Jewish and other minority communities to host cultural events, workshops, and open houses to bridge gaps in understanding with broader Australian society.

Preventing Polarisation

This act of terror also highlights the risks of polarisation. Knee-jerk reactions and divisive rhetoric can exacerbate tensions, pushing communities further apart. It is vital that leaders, educators, and media outlets take a measured approach, focusing on unity rather than assigning blame or escalating fears. Cultural Education offers a pathway to prevent polarisation by teaching individuals how to engage in difficult conversations with respect and understanding, creating environments where diversity is seen as a strength rather than a threat.

Aspirations and Outcomes

A society shaped by robust Cultural Education would see fewer incidents of hatred and violence. By embedding principles of empathy, respect, and inclusion into every facet of public life - schools, workplaces, media, and governance - Australia can work toward a future where acts of terror against any community are unthinkable. The Ripponlea Synagogue attack serves as a sobering call to action, urging governments, educators, and communities to prioritise education as a tool for dismantling hatred and establishing a cohesive, inclusive nation.

Addressing Domestic and Family Violence Through Cultural Education

Domestic and family violence (DFV) remains one of the most pressing social and mental health issues in Australia, disproportionately impacting women and children, particularly in CALD communities. For example, within my own community, DFV arises from a complex interplay of cultural expectations, patriarchal norms, and systemic barriers, making it both a community and national issue.

While the foundational teachings of Sikhism emphasise gender equality and mutual respect, cultural practices such as traditional Indian/Pakistan practices like dowry demands and entrenched patriarchal attitudes have overshadowed these values. Survivors of DFV, particularly women, often face immense societal pressure to remain silent due to the collectivist nature of these communities, where family reputation and "*behzti*" (dishonour) are prioritised over individual safety.

Mental Health Consequences of DFV

The psychological toll of DFV is devastating. Survivors frequently endure depression, anxiety, post-traumatic stress disorder (PTSD), and even suicidal ideation. Amongst Sikh women for example, these challenges are compounded by cultural stigma, which discourages them from seeking help, and a lack of culturally sensitive mental health services. Research by Scroll.in (2023) has highlighted how DFV survivors often feel trapped, with no safe avenues for emotional or psychological support.

This isolation exacerbates their mental health struggles and creates intergenerational cycles of trauma within families.

Nationally, data underscores the severe impact of DFV on mental health. A report by *1800RESPECT* revealed that women from CALD backgrounds are overrepresented in calls for assistance, yet they face unique barriers to accessing support, including language difficulties, lack of trust in institutions, and fear of visa repercussions.

Structural and Systemic Barriers in CALD Communities

For migrants from CALD communities, DFV is often exacerbated by structural barriers. Language barriers, financial dependency - especially for women on spousal visas - and cultural isolation create significant hurdles for survivors seeking help. Many are unaware of available support services, while mainstream organisations often lack the cultural competence needed to provide effective and empathetic assistance, leaving victims feeling alienated and misunderstood.

Within some CALD communities, cultural dynamics further discourage survivors from taking action. Concerns about "disgrace" or bringing "shame" to the family or community often pressure individuals to remain silent, perpetuating cycles of abuse. Religious leaders, while occasionally vocal about women's rights, frequently avoid directly addressing DFV to maintain harmony within male-dominated congregations. This reluctance sustains harmful practices and stalls meaningful progress.

Cultural Education programs can play a pivotal role in addressing these challenges by tapping into awareness of egalitarian values, equipping communities with tools to move from destructive traditions to constructive practices, and building culturally sensitive support networks. By bridging gaps in understanding and access, these initiatives empower survivors to seek help without fear of cultural or systemic backlash. Early education initiatives that incorporate lessons on emotional intelligence, healthy relationships, and mutual respect can instil values that counteract DFV.

National Implications and Broader Relevance

By equipping community leaders, educators, and policymakers with the tools to encourage open dialogue and provide support, Australia can move closer to its vision of equality and cohesion.

Case Studies: Promising Practices

1. **Australia's Multicultural Centre for Women's Health**
   The Centre offers culturally tailored workshops for CALD communities, focusing on gender equality, family violence prevention, and mental health awareness. By engaging community leaders and providing resources in multiple languages, the program has successfully reached isolated groups and reduced stigma around seeking help.
2. **Canada's Immigrant Women's Centre**
   In Canada, similar challenges have been addressed through the Immigrant Women's Centre, which combines Cultural Education with practical support, such as legal aid and language training. This holistic approach not only helps survivors escape abusive situations but also equips them to rebuild their lives.

3. **Victoria's Free from Violence Strategy**
   The Victorian government's initiative includes programs that integrate Cultural Education with DFV prevention, targeting CALD communities through schools, workplaces, and faith-based organisations. By addressing the cultural dimensions of DFV, the strategy aims to implement long-term societal change.

Broader Implications for Australian Society

The issue of DFV in CALD communities reflects broader challenges faced by Australia's multicultural society. The Scanlon Foundation's (2024) Social Cohesion Report highlights how economic pressures and housing insecurity exacerbate feelings of isolation and diminish trust in government institutions. These factors contribute to a sense of disempowerment among vulnerable populations, creating an environment where DFV can thrive.

Cultural Education, when integrated into national policies and school curricula, can serve as a preventive measure. By equipping individuals with the tools to recognise and challenge harmful norms, Cultural Education can reduce the prevalence of DFV while promoting mental health and social cohesion.

Practical Recommendations

1. **Culturally Tailored DFV Education Programs**
   Develop workshops and resources that address DFV within the context of specific cultural values, such as equality and respect. These programs should involve community leaders, educators, and

86

survivors to ensure cultural relevance and authenticity (Roots of Empathy 2021). Each community or faith group would have its own idiosyncrasies, which will need to be taken into consideration. For example the issue of equality between male and female in Islam.

2. **Integration into School Curricula**
   Introduce age-appropriate lessons on healthy relationships, emotional intelligence, and respect for diversity into primary and secondary education. This early intervention can help prevent biases and promote gender equality from a young age.

3. **Training for Service Providers**
   Enhance the cultural competence of DFV service providers through targeted training programs. This will ensure that survivors from CALD backgrounds receive support that is empathetic, relevant, and effective (Weddle et al.2024).

4. **Community-Led Advocacy**
   Empower survivors and community leaders to advocate for change through storytelling, public awareness campaigns, and collaboration with policymakers. These efforts can challenge stigma and foster a culture of accountability (Deloitte 2021).

Addressing DFV requires a multifaceted approach that combines Cultural Education, community engagement, and systemic reform. By integrating these elements, Australia can create a society where all individuals - regardless of cultural background - are protected, respected and empowered to live free from violence.

Conclusion: Building Foundations for Empathy and Unity

Early education serves as the cornerstone of a society that values empathy, resilience, and inclusion. Addressing biases and cultivating cultural awareness from an early age lays the groundwork for a future where diversity is not only celebrated but understood and embraced. This chapter has highlighted the transformative potential of Cultural Education in shaping individuals who are equipped to navigate and contribute positively to a multicultural society.

The recent synagogue attack in Melbourne underscores the societal costs of neglecting cultural cohesion and awareness. Incidents like these are not isolated but are symptomatic of broader societal divides that demand urgent attention. Embedding Cultural Education into schools, workplaces, and communities becomes a critical tool for dismantling prejudice and fortifying unity.

Equally vital is addressing systemic challenges such as bullying, domestic and family violence, and the gaps created by misaligned faith-based initiatives. These issues not only harm individuals but also fracture the social fabric, making it imperative to adopt a holistic approach to Cultural Education - one that incorporates emotional intelligence, resilience-building, and the creation of psychologically safe spaces.

Mindfulness and life skills training are essential components of this framework, empowering young people to manage stress, develop empathy, and understand their own biases. When children are taught to see themselves and others through a lens of shared humanity, they become ambassadors of unity in their families, schools, and broader communities.

The pathway to this vision requires a collective effort. Policymakers must ensure curricula reflect Australia's diversity and address the unique challenges faced by its multicultural population. Educators need the tools and training to create inclusive environments that encourage critical thinking and challenge stereotypes. Families and communities play an equally important role in reinforcing these values at home and in daily interactions.

The stakes could not be higher. Events like the synagogue attack serve as stark reminders of the consequences of inaction. Other direct consequences of biases ingrained in childhood impact the broader workforce, indirectly influencing skilled migrants' experiences. Australia is already seeing more "reverse migration" to countries like Korea, China and India, losing the skills we need. However, through intentional, well-designed Cultural Education initiatives, we can move beyond these divides. By bolstering empathy, resilience, and unity, we can build a future where every individual - regardless of their background - feels valued, respected, and empowered to thrive. This is not merely an aspiration but a necessity for a society that seeks to turn diversity into its greatest strength.

Chapter 6
A Roadmap for Building Inclusive Societies

Building an inclusive society is a collective endeavour that requires efforts from policymakers, educators, corporations, and communities. Cultural diversity enriches society, but inclusion demands intentional action, systemic changes, and accountability. This chapter explores practical strategies for advancing inclusivity, supported by global case studies, data-driven insights, and actionable recommendations tailored to the Australian context.

Case Study:
A poignant example of Cultural Education establishing psychological safety and reconciliation took place during a women's gathering my mum and I organised (as part of the Womens' Interfaith Network Foundation of which mum was the founder and president at the time), with the Yorta Yorta women of Barmah Forest, Victoria, and the Brigidine Sisters from Echuca. After getting the women to sit down, I created a psychologically safe space and asked, the late Aunty Walda Blow, a matriarch of the Yorta Yorta people to start. She began the session by sharing her harrowing experiences growing up on the Cummeragunja Reserve. Her account of the stolen generation - of children, including her cousins, being taken as 'half castes' or 'quarter castes' - was raw and deeply personal. She described the community's desperate strategies, including escape routes, early warning systems, and hiding places to counter the arrival of "white officers" in the black-painted government cars, who snatched their

children never to be seen again, the unimaginable pain of losing them forever.

The Brigidine Sisters, seated across the circle, responded with shock and disbelief. They shared their own childhood memories of being told by the church that they were "saving" these children from neglect and abuse. Their narratives, shaped by the institutions they trusted, clashed profoundly with Aunty Walda's lived reality. Yet, in the safety of this yarning circle, their stories did not create division - they opened the door to empathy and mutual understanding.

By the end of the session, tears had been shed, hugs exchanged, and a deep sense of connection forged. This gathering was the beginning of years of collaboration between the Yorta Yorta Nation and the Brigidine Sisters, who worked together for the betterment of First Nations communities in the region.

Mandatory Cultural Competency Training
Introduce mandatory cultural awareness training for educators, public service workers, and law enforcement. Studies show that trained professionals are better equipped to interact with diverse communities, reducing instances of discrimination and bias.

Incorporate Cultural Education in the National Curriculum
The Australian national curriculum could include more dedicated modules on Cultural Education, covering First Nations histories, migration patterns, and global diversity. By making this a core part of education from early childhood to secondary school, future generations will grow up with an ingrained respect for diversity (ACARA 2023).

Annual National Cultural Cohesion Index
Establish a government-backed Cultural Cohesion Index
to assess the effectiveness of Cultural Education and
inclusion policies across states and territories. This index
could be modelled on Canada's annual Multiculturalism
Report, providing a transparent review of societal
progress and areas needing attention (Porter 2004).

Transparency and Accountability in Funding

Rethinking Funding Models
The Victorian Multicultural Commission (VMC) and local
governments currently allocate funding to individual
communities for cultural celebrations, infrastructure, and
other initiatives. While these efforts build community
pride and enable cultural preservation, they can
inadvertently reinforce silos by keeping groups separate
rather than promoting broader integration. For instance,
the recent Indian Community Infrastructure Fund (ICIF),
designed to support Indian communities in upgrading
their facilities, highlights the importance of empowering
specific cultural groups. However, initiatives like this risk
being perceived as exclusive, potentially alienating other
communities who may feel overlooked or unsupported.

To elicit true inclusivity, funding should focus on cross-
cultural initiatives that encourage shared experiences and
mutual understanding. Programs that bring together
multiple communities - such as intercultural festivals,
collaborative community spaces, or joint leadership
development initiatives - can help bridge divides and
create a more cohesive multicultural society. This
approach does not diminish the significance of cultural
preservation but ensures that it is balanced with
opportunities for collaboration and unity across diverse
groups.

- **Shared Festivals:** Events that celebrate multiple cultures in unified settings, promoting dialogue and mutual understanding.
- **Interfaith Dialogues:** Forums where representatives from different faiths can discuss shared values and societal challenges. Then take them back to their individual communities as part of the program and report back with surveys, feedback forms, data etc.
- **Cultural Exchange Programs:** Fund programs that allow students and communities to experience diverse traditions firsthand, building bridges across cultural divides. These must also create psychologically safe spaces where students / teachers are not ridiculed or judged for asking questions.

Auditing and Reporting

Introduce an independent auditing body to oversee how multicultural funds are distributed and their measurable outcomes. Clear, transparent reporting on how these funds benefit both individual communities and broader social cohesion will ensure accountability.

Immigration Reform

Australia's immigration system must balance national security with inclusion. Policies that support refugees and skilled migrants can enhance societal and economic resilience.

Canada's Express Entry System

Canada's points-based immigration system prioritises skilled migrants, promoting economic integration while fostering inclusivity (Porter 2004).

Australia's Refugee Intake

While Australia admits 11,000–14,000 refugees annually, critics argue that the system must strike a better balance. The over-assistance of refugees at the expense of addressing critical issues such as homelessness and the housing crisis can foster resentment among vulnerable Australians, undermining social cohesion (UNHCR 2023).

Equitable Resource Allocation

Reallocate resources to ensure equitable support for both refugees and disadvantaged Australians. This includes prioritising affordable housing, mental health services, and job training for all citizens, regardless of background.

National Dialogue on Immigration

Launch a national dialogue on immigration policies to address public concerns and reduce misinformation. This could include town halls, online forums, and public education campaigns to build trust and ensure transparency in how immigration policies are shaped and implemented.

The Threat of Reverse Migration

Australia has long positioned itself as a destination for skilled migrants, relying on their expertise to address workforce shortages and drive innovation. However, a growing trend of "reverse migration" threatens this strategy. Skilled migrants, who arrive with qualifications, experience, and ambition, are increasingly returning to their countries of origin after encountering systemic biases, stereotypes, and workplace barriers that limit their upward mobility (Park 2010).

Despite excelling in their roles and undertaking professional development to align with Australian standards, many migrants find themselves overlooked for senior positions. This stagnation stems from unconscious biases within corporate and government sectors, where leadership roles often remain disproportionately inaccessible to individuals from CALD backgrounds. These structural inequities undermine Australia's global reputation as a land of opportunity.

Reverse migration is not solely driven by career stagnation. Many migrants cite concerns about their children's education and value-based learning as reasons to leave. They observe that while Australia prioritises individualism, their home countries often offer a stronger emphasis on academic excellence and values-based education, which align more closely with their aspirations for their families.

If unaddressed, reverse migration could lead to a significant brain drain, with Australia losing top talent to countries that provide better opportunities and cultural alignment. Policymakers must take this issue seriously, embedding Cultural Education across all sectors to dismantle biases, create pathways for career advancement, and build inclusive environments where skilled migrants can thrive.

Strategies for Educators

Education remains the most powerful tool for dismantling biases and cultivating a culture of inclusivity from an early age.

1. Professional Development for Teachers

To effectively manage diverse classrooms, teachers must be equipped with the tools, training, and awareness necessary to promote inclusivity without inadvertently imposing their own biases. Education is a powerful platform for shaping young minds, but it also requires immense responsibility to ensure that personal or political views do not cloud the learning environment.

Recent events, such as Victorian teachers endorsing a "week of action" to show solidarity with Palestinians, highlight the complexities of balancing professional responsibilities with personal beliefs. The Australian Education Union's Victorian branch encouraged teachers to visibly support Palestinians by wearing keffiyehs or pro-Palestinian badges. While advocacy for global issues is important, bringing overt political positions into classrooms risks alienating students and their families, especially those from Jewish or other affected communities. This can exacerbate divisions and potentially contribute to incidents such as the recent anti-Semitic attacks in Melbourne, fostering distrust and tension within already diverse and sensitive educational settings (SBS News 2024).

Teachers must be trained to navigate these complex dynamics, ensuring their classrooms remain neutral spaces for learning and critical thinking. Professional development programs should emphasise cultural awareness, the management of personal biases, and strategies for facilitating open yet respectful discussions on global and domestic issues. This includes understanding how their actions and language can inadvertently influence students' perceptions, reinforcing stereotypes, or creating divisions.

Additionally, education departments should provide clear guidelines on how political or cultural issues should be addressed in schools. Teachers need support in understanding the line between supporting informed global citizenship and inadvertently endorsing particular political stances that could alienate or harm students.

By prioritising comprehensive professional development that includes cultural responsiveness, emotional intelligence, and political neutrality, schools can ensure that classrooms remain inclusive, empowering spaces where all students feel respected and valued.

Teachers also need to hold space - psychologically safe spaces that are physically, emotionally, and mentally secure. This means creating an environment where students feel free to express themselves, share experiences, and explore cultural differences without fear of racial vilification or judgment. By creating such an atmosphere, teachers can help students reflect on their own biases and stereotypes, encouraging personal growth and a deeper understanding of diversity.

Canada's Anti-Racism Training: Canadian teachers undergo mandatory training on cultural responsiveness and anti-racism, preparing them to address biases in the classroom (CCDI 2021).

Australia's Opportunity: While Australia's curriculum integrates Aboriginal and Torres Strait Islander histories, teacher training on these topics is inconsistent.

Inclusive Curriculum Design

Curricula must reflect the diverse histories, cultures, and contributions of all Australians.

- **Finland's Holistic Model**: Finland's education system integrates multicultural education into subjects like history, geography, and literature, emphasising empathy and global citizenship (FNAE 2021).
- **Australia Day in Schools**: Teaching Australia Day as a dual narrative - acknowledging the struggles of First Nations people while celebrating

the contributions of immigrants can generate a more nuanced understanding of national identity.

Safe School Environments

Bullying, particularly racial bullying, remains a significant issue in Australian schools.

- **Beyond Blue Report**: Approximately 27% of Australian students report experiencing racial bullying, leading to mental health challenges and lower academic outcomes. Programs like Japan's early emphasis on values-based education could serve as a model for Australian schools to instil respect and empathy from the outset (Beyond Blue 2023).

Opportunities for Change

1. Honest Dialogue
Australia must advocate for open discussions about racism and inclusivity without fear of political backlash.
- **Council Campaign Reflection**: My personal experience during the Casey Council campaign highlighted the pervasive nature of conscious and unconscious biases. Racially charged attacks on my campaign boards, covered extensively in the media, underscored the need for systemic change at every level.

2. Mandating English Proficiency
While controversial, mandating basic English literacy for long-term Centrelink recipients (for example) could improve social mobility and integration. Incentivising language acquisition through free courses and support systems would create a win-win scenario.

3. Funding Cross-Cultural Initiatives

Redirecting funds from individual cultural celebrations to shared events could nurture greater understanding and unity.

4. Enhancing Workforce Skills

Investing in skilled programs (including cross and up-skilling) for unemployed individuals ensures that government support is empowering rather than enabling.

5. Leveraging Australia's Diversity

With nearly half of its population born overseas or with at least one foreign-born parent, Australia is uniquely positioned to harness its diversity as a strength. However, this requires moving beyond tokenism to genuine representation and inclusion.

Breaking the "Ghetto Mentality"

The VMC funding model, while undoubtedly well-intentioned, risks inadvertently perpetuating a "ghetto mentality." This approach, which emphasises supporting individual cultural communities through siloed initiatives, often reinforces cultural insularity rather than encouraging integration into a broader, unified Australian identity. A critical analysis suggests that while celebrating cultural heritage is vital, funding should also prioritise cross-cultural initiatives that promote mutual understanding, shared experiences, and the collective adoption of Australian values.

Melbourne has become a case study in the challenges of such an approach. For instance, in the City of Casey, the Afghan community is concentrated heavily in certain areas. While this clustering can provide much-needed social support and a sense of belonging for those who have fled war-torn regions, it simultaneously creates barriers to integration. Language acquisition, a cornerstone of successful settlement and inclusion, is deprioritised in these self-contained communities. Women, particularly stay-at-home mothers, often lack the incentive or opportunity to learn English, further isolating them from broader Australian society.

This insularity can inadvertently fuel tensions. Conversations with local educators, librarians, and community workers during my campaign revealed unsettling patterns. For example, a female librarian shared that groups of Afghan boys frequently display blatant disrespect toward female staff but show deference to male staff members. Similar sentiments were echoed by teachers, who, although reluctant to voice these concerns publicly, noted cultural behaviours among male students that clash with Australian norms of gender equality and respect.

This dynamic instigates resentment among the broader Australian population, who may perceive these behaviours as a rejection of shared national values. Instead of developing unity, this "ghetto mentality" nurtures mutual distrust, stereotypes, and biases. It risks exacerbating societal divisions and creating conditions similar to those seen in England, where unchecked segregation and lack of meaningful dialogue have led to heightened nationalism and Islamophobia.

To address this, Australia must adopt a more proactive approach. Funding models need to shift from supporting only community-specific celebrations to initiatives that encourage cross-cultural interaction and education. Programs should focus on shared goals, such as women's empowerment, children's education, and community-wide activities that unite diverse groups.

Furthermore, cultural orientation programs should emphasise not just language acquisition but also Australian values like gender equality, respect, and inclusivity. These efforts must be implemented in a way that is respectful and empowering, ensuring that communities feel supported rather than alienated. Without decisive action, Australia risks forming divisions rather than unity, undoing decades of progress toward multicultural harmony.

Social Cohesion and Multicultural Integration: Insights from the Scanlon Foundation.
Australia prides itself on being one of the most multicultural nations globally, with its diversity often heralded as a strength. However, the Scanlon Foundation report (2024) highlights underlying challenges that risk undermining this cohesion. While social cohesion has remained stable over the past year - despite persistent economic pressures and global tensions - growing concerns about immigration and religious tolerance signal a need for urgent action.

The report measures social cohesion through five key indicators: worth, social justice and inclusion, acceptance, belonging, and political participation. These dimensions provide a nuanced lens through which to assess Australia's progress and challenges in building a unified society. In 2024, the overall sense of belonging remained steady, scoring 78, the same as in 2023. Yet, this surface stability masks significant tensions.

Almost half of Australians (49%) now believe immigration levels are too high, a stark rise from 33% in 2023. Importantly, this sentiment is driven less by opposition to diversity and more by concerns over economic pressures, housing shortages, and safety. This distinction underscores the need for nuanced policies that address these root causes without fuelling anti-immigrant sentiment.

Faith and Religious Acceptance
Another alarming trend is the decline in positive attitudes toward all major faith groups. In 2024, only 37% of Australians expressed a somewhat or very positive view of Christians, down from 42% in 2023. Negative attitudes toward Muslims have risen sharply, with one-third of respondents reporting unfavourable views, a seven-point increase from the previous year. Similarly, negative perceptions of Jewish people increased from 9% to 13%.

The report attributes part of these shifts to global events, such as the Gaza conflict, which have intensified religious and cultural divisions within Australian communities. These trends highlight the critical role of Cultural Education in countering stereotypes and nurturing understanding. Programs that engage communities in shared learning and dialogue can help bridge divides exacerbated by international crises and local biases.

Economic Strain and the Erosion of Belonging
The link between economic strain and social cohesion is stark. The report finds that 41% of Australians now describe themselves as "poor or struggling to pay bills." These financial pressures erode trust in government and institutions, reduce the sense of belonging, and weaken acceptance of diversity. When individuals face economic hardship, they are more likely to retreat into cultural silos, perpetuating the "ghetto mentality" discussed earlier in this chapter.

Addressing the Root Causes
The findings reinforce the urgency of addressing economic and housing challenges as part of Australia's

broader strategy for social cohesion. Policies must ensure that multiculturalism is not only celebrated but also supported through tangible measures such as affordable housing, access to education, and employment opportunities for all Australians. Furthermore, integrating Cultural Education into school curricula can play a pivotal role in breaking down misconceptions about immigration and religious diversity.

A Path Forward
The 2024 Scanlon Foundation report serves as both a cautionary tale and a call to action. While Australians overwhelmingly agree (85%) that multiculturalism has been good for the nation, the report underscores the fragility of this consensus. Maintaining social cohesion requires sustained efforts to address economic inequalities, instil cross-cultural understanding, and promote inclusive narratives.

By restructuring funding models and encouraging initiatives that bring diverse communities together, Australia can ensure that its multicultural identity remains a source of strength. The five measures of social cohesion outlined in the report - worth, social justice and inclusion, acceptance, belonging, and political participation - offer a robust framework for policymakers, educators, and community leaders to guide their efforts. In doing so, Australia can move closer to a society where diversity is not just tolerated but embraced as a cornerstone of national identity.

Political Representation and Cultural Education

Advancing Women in Leadership: Lessons from Women for Elections

As part of my campaign for the City of Casey Council, I had the privilege of connecting with *Women for Elections* (WFE), an Australian organisation dedicated to inspiring, equipping, and sustaining women to stand for and thrive in public office. Their work underscores the importance of gender representation at all levels of government, offering workshops, resources, and support networks that empower women from diverse backgrounds to step into leadership roles confidently.

Through WFE, I encountered women from across Australia standing for or thinking about standing for local, state, and federal elections, representing political parties and running as independents. These sessions revealed not only the courage of these women but also the systemic barriers they face. Many women, particularly those from CALD communities, focused their campaign narratives on advocating for their specific communities. While this is admirable, it often highlights a key gap in understanding the broader role of government - to represent all constituents regardless of race, gender, ethnicity, age, or ability.

My campaign intentionally deviated from this norm. While my Sikh heritage is central to who I am, I made it clear that my platform was about inclusivity - representing all constituents in my ward equally. This approach resonated with many voters, but it also highlighted a structural issue: a majority portion of elected officials in the City of Casey were from Anglo-Saxon backgrounds, not reflecting the multicultural mix of the constituents and reflecting a lack of diversity in leadership that is not unique to my ward.

This experience underscores the urgent need for Cultural Education programs that extend beyond promoting diversity to actively promoting understanding about what it means to lead in a multicultural society. Initiatives like WFE must be complemented by broader efforts to educate CALD candidates about representing all Australians, encouraging narratives that unite rather than segregate communities. By supporting women across cultural and linguistic divides, organisations like WFE are laying the groundwork for a future where leadership is more representative of Australia's rich diversity.

Conclusion: Calling a Spade a Spade

Building truly inclusive societies requires more than surface-level gestures or well-meaning platitudes; it demands a willingness to confront uncomfortable truths with honesty, transparency, and decisive action. "Calling a spade a spade" means naming the issues clearly and without sugar-coating, recognising both the successes and failures in promoting inclusion. Australia, often praised for its multiculturalism, must face the challenges that remain deeply rooted in its policies, communities, and institutions.

A multifaceted approach is essential. Mandating comprehensive Cultural Education in schools is a foundational step, but it must be supported by policies that restructure funding models to prevent the reinforcement of silos and ghetto mentalities. Programs and initiatives should focus on integration without erasing cultural identity - empowering communities to celebrate their heritage while embracing Australian values of fairness, respect, and equality. This includes addressing uncomfortable issues such as gender inequities within specific communities, linguistic barriers, and the need for all Australians to feel represented in national narratives.

Global and local examples show that inclusivity is not just a moral imperative - it is critical for social harmony, economic growth, and national pride. However, tokenistic gestures must give way to policies that hold all stakeholders accountable, enhancing cross-cultural interaction and empowering communities to actively participate in shaping a shared future.

By breaking down barriers to integration, promoting genuine social cohesion, and addressing systemic biases, Australia can set a precedent for inclusivity that is rooted in equity and shared prosperity. Only by calling a spade a spade can we move forward, ensuring that every individual feels empowered to contribute meaningfully to the society in which they live.

Chapter 7
Cultural Education as a Catalyst in Creating Psychologically Safe Environments

Cultural Education plays a pivotal role in establishing psychologically safe environments where individuals feel secure to express their identities, perspectives, and experiences without fear of judgment or reprisal. It addresses the nuanced complexities of multicultural societies, offering tools to navigate cultural differences, challenge stereotypes, and build connections. This chapter delves into the transformative power of Cultural Education in promoting inclusion, corporate creativity, and equitable policymaking, while tackling hard truths about societal challenges.

The Need for Psychological Safety in Diverse Societies

Psychological safety refers to an environment where individuals feel valued, respected, and free to contribute without fear of embarrassment or rejection. In diverse societies, cultural misunderstandings and biases can undermine this safety, leading to exclusion and alienation.

Smith's conceptual model, Foucault's Oscillation (2024). underscores the role of reflective practice in building culturally safe environments. This aligns with this book's advocacy for proactive Cultural Education to dismantle biases and promote psychological safety across societal structures.

Challenging Stereotypes and Misconceptions

Cultural Education equips individuals with the tools to identify and confront stereotypes. Stereotypes, whether conscious or unconscious, perpetuate systemic inequities and harm marginalised communities.

- **Pauline Hanson and One Nation's Narrative:** Pauline Hanson's rhetoric often highlights divisive language against minority groups, portraying multiculturalism as a threat. Her remarks, such as opposing the burqa in Parliament, exemplify how cultural ignorance instigates division. Countering such narratives requires education that emphasises the contributions of diverse communities while dismantling myths about incompatibility (ABC News 2023).

- **Case Study: Afghan Refugee Communities in Australia:** Afghanistan's war-torn history has led to waves of migration to Australia. However, the trauma of survival in conflict zones, coupled with cultural norms that often marginalise women, creates unique challenges. Initiatives such as the Afghan Women's Organisation in Sydney promote gender equity and integration by offering cultural orientation programs that include discussions on Australian values.

Amplifying Marginalised Voices

Cultural Education provides platforms for marginalised groups to share their narratives, forging empathy and dismantling bias.

Policing and Cultural Nuances: In some cultures, avoiding eye contact is a sign of respect, yet in Australia, it is often interpreted as deceit. Police forces require training in cultural nuances to prevent misinterpretation. The Queensland Police Service has introduced the Cross-Cultural Liaison Officer program to address such gaps, significantly reducing community tensions.

Cultural Education in Corporate Environments

Diversity without inclusion is an empty gesture. Cultural Education in workplaces goes beyond tokenism to create truly inclusive environments where employees from all backgrounds thrive.

Encouraging Open Communication

When employees feel psychologically safe, they are more likely to share innovative ideas and collaborate effectively.

Case Study: SAP's Autism at Work Program: SAP actively recruits neurodiverse individuals, including those on the autism spectrum, and trains teams on cultural and psychological safety to integrate them effectively. This approach has boosted productivity and innovation (SAP 2022).

Addressing Gender Inequities and Cultural Biases

Gender biases, particularly in male-dominated cultures, often spill over into Australian workplaces, creating barriers to achieving psychological safety for all employees. These biases can manifest in subtle ways, from dismissive or patronising attitudes to overt discrimination, and can be exacerbated by initiatives that, while well-intentioned, are perceived as tokenistic or misaligned with organisational culture.

The Complexity of Gender Equity Targets

In efforts to combat gender inequity, many organisations have adopted initiatives like mandating a 50/50 male-to-female representation on boards and in leadership roles. While such measures are designed to level the playing field, they can sometimes lead to unintended consequences. For women placed in these roles, there is often an underlying uncertainty: **"Am I here because of my abilities, or because I tick the box?"** This self-doubt can undermine their confidence, diminishing their ability to lead effectively and eroding their sense of psychological safety.

Similarly, male colleagues and subordinates may question the legitimacy of these appointments, assuming that merit played a secondary role to gender quotas. This perception harbours resentment and resistance, undermining workplace cohesion and creating additional hurdles for women leaders to overcome. The very policies aimed at promoting equity can inadvertently reinforce biases, as they are viewed as imposing artificial constraints rather than rewarding genuine capability.

Creating a Culture of Genuine Equity

Addressing these challenges requires more than simply meeting numerical targets; it demands a cultural shift that emphasises competence, transparency, and mutual respect. Organizations must:

1. **Ensure Clear Selection Processes:** Leadership appointments should be based on clear, transparent criteria that emphasise skills, experience, and potential. Communicating these criteria to all employees helps to mitigate perceptions of tokenism.

2. **Build Confidence in Female Leaders:** Mentorship programs and leadership training tailored to women can provide the support needed to navigate male-dominated environments, boosting confidence and capability.

3. **Educate and Engage All Employees:** Cultural Education programs that address unconscious biases can help male colleagues understand and respect the contributions of their female peers, while dismantling stereotypes that undermine workplace relationships.

4. **Focus on Outcomes, Not Quotas:** While targets can serve as a guide, the ultimate aim should be to workplaces where all employees a workplace culture where gender equity arises naturally from inclusivity, fair policies, and opportunities for all employees to thrive.

Psychological Safety for All

For gender equity initiatives to succeed, they must align with broader efforts to create psychologically safe workplaces. Employees, regardless of gender, must feel valued for their contributions, free from the fear of judgment or bias. This requires encouraging open dialogue, providing support for diverse leadership styles, and emphasising collaboration over competition.

By addressing gender inequities with a nuanced, culturally aware approach, organisations can move beyond tick-box solutions to form workplaces where all employees - female and male - feel empowered to lead, contribute, and innovate.

Global Comparisons: In Saudi Arabia, recent reforms have improved women's rights, yet deep-seated gender biases remain. Similarly, some migrant communities in Australia bring cultural norms that marginalise women. Programs like the Women in Leadership initiative by the Commonwealth Bank promote gender equity by providing mentorship and leadership opportunities for women of all backgrounds (CBA 2023).

Educational Systems and Cultural Integration

Australia's curriculum is secular, but it must also be responsive to the cultural diversity within its classrooms. Global citizenship, values education, and Cultural Education are indispensable for building a cohesive society.

Case Study: Finland's Multilingual Education Policies: Finland offers Swedish, Finnish, and English as mandatory languages, promoting multilingualism and integration. This policy has enhanced social cohesion and empowered migrant communities (FNAE 2023).

Life. Be in it.: Promoting Active Lives and Social Cohesion

Australia's iconic *Life. Be in it.* campaign, featuring the relatable character Norm, is a quintessential example of how cultural initiatives can promote health, inclusion, and social cohesion. Launched in the late 1970s, the campaign encouraged Australians to "get up, get out, and get active" in an era when sedentary lifestyles were becoming increasingly prevalent. Norm, the archetypal "average Aussie," satirized the laid-back Australian attitude towards fitness, inspiring people of all ages and backgrounds to engage in physical activity.
The campaign's relevance extends beyond health - it highlights the unifying potential of Cultural Education.

In a conversation with Dr. Colin Benjamin, the Director General of *Life. Be in it.*, he articulated how the campaign not only promoted physical well-being but also emphasised social cohesion. Dr. Benjamin noted that effective cultural frameworks must provide people with "a sense of who they are and their role in society." He linked this to Julia Rotter's theory of social learning, which posits that individuals learn their roles and behaviours through observation and interaction within their social environments.

Norm's character resonated deeply because he represented an everyman - a "normal" Australian who could inspire others to break free from passive routines and engage with their communities. As Norm might have quipped in character, "Culture? I got good culture. I get my culture from my telly!" This tongue-in-cheek observation underscores the importance of role models and positive reinforcement in shaping cultural norms. Dr. Benjamin emphasised that cultural initiatives must steer individuals away from negative peer influences and create pathways toward responsibility and inclusivity.

Teaching Australian Values: A Pillar of Cultural Education

Australia's national identity is deeply rooted in its core values, which reflect the principles and practices that have helped shape the country into a secure, prosperous, and peaceful place to live. These values are integral to maintaining a cohesive society, instilling a sense of belonging, and ensuring equality of opportunity for all. Teaching these values to both migrants and children is not merely an exercise in education; it is a way of preserving and enhancing the essence of what it means to be Australian.

Mateship

Mateship is one of the most defining aspects of Australian culture. Rooted in camaraderie, solidarity, and loyalty, mateship signifies standing by your friends and neighbours through good times and bad. It is about looking out for each other, offering help without expecting anything in return, and treating others as equals. Historically, mateship emerged from the hardships faced by early settlers and the camaraderie of soldiers during wartime, becoming a powerful symbol of the Australian spirit.

In modern Australia, mateship is visible in everyday acts of kindness, community support during natural disasters like bushfires and floods, and the collective resilience shown during challenges such as the COVID-19 pandemic. Teaching mateship creates empathy, compassion, and a sense of responsibility towards others, building stronger communities.

Fairness

Fairness underpins Australia's belief in equality and justice. It reflects the idea that everyone deserves a "fair go", irrespective of their background, ethnicity, religion, physical ability or socioeconomic status. This value is enshrined in Australian laws, which promote equal rights and opportunities for all citizens, and it is a guiding principle in schools, workplaces, and community practices.

Teaching fairness encourages inclusivity and an appreciation of diversity. It helps children and migrants understand that discrimination and prejudice have no place in Australian society. By upholding fairness, Australia strengthens its democratic foundations and ensures that every individual feels valued and respected.

Larrikin Spirit

The larrikin spirit represents Australia's distinctive sense of humour, irreverence, and playfulness. While it often conveys a carefree and cheeky attitude, it also reflects resilience, resourcefulness, and the ability to find joy even in adversity. Historically, this spirit was embodied by the bushrangers, diggers, and pioneers who faced significant challenges, including belligerent authoritarianism with grit and wit.

Teaching the larrikin spirit is about nurturing creativity, optimism, and a positive outlook on life. It encourages individuals to question authority constructively, embrace individuality, and approach life with a sense of humour and humility.

Sportsmanship

Australians are known for their love of sports, which is deeply embedded in the national psyche. Sportsmanship embodies qualities such as teamwork, respect for opponents, perseverance, and celebrating the joy of participation over mere victory. Whether it's cricket, rugby, Australian Rules Football, netball, soccer or athletics, sports unite communities, break down barriers, and create shared experiences.

Teaching sportsmanship instils discipline, mutual respect, and a commitment to fair play. It also helps individuals develop resilience, as they learn to handle both triumphs and setbacks with grace. This value strengthens Australia's reputation as a nation that values healthy competition, collaboration, and community spirit.

Freedom

Freedom is a cornerstone of Australian values, encompassing the right to speak, believe, and live as one chooses within the boundaries of the law. Australia's democratic system ensures freedom of expression, religion, and association, creating an environment where people can thrive without fear of persecution.

Teaching freedom highlights the importance of respecting others' rights and embracing diversity of thought and belief. It encourages individuals to appreciate the privileges they enjoy while understanding the responsibilities that come with such liberties.

Equality of Opportunity

Equality of opportunity is a fundamental principle in Australian society. It reflects the belief that everyone, regardless of their background, should have access to education, employment, health care, and other resources necessary to succeed. This value promotes social mobility, inclusivity, and the pursuit of excellence.

Teaching this value helps children and migrants understand that hard work and determination can open doors to success. It also underscores the importance of creating systems that support those in need, ensuring that everyone has a fair chance to achieve their potential.

Respect

Respect is a value that underlies every aspect of Australian life. It involves honouring the rights, beliefs, and cultures of others while recognising and appreciating differences. Respect is integral to developing social harmony and reducing conflicts, making it a vital part of multicultural Australia.

Teaching respect cultivates empathy, understanding, and acceptance. It helps individuals navigate a diverse society with sensitivity and ensures that interactions are grounded in dignity and mutual regard.

Responsibility

Responsibility refers to the duty each individual has to contribute positively to society, protect the environment, and uphold the law. It is about being accountable for one's actions and making choices that benefit both oneself and the broader community.

Teaching responsibility empowers individuals to take ownership of their lives and understand the impact of their decisions. It also reinforces the importance of civic participation, encouraging people to engage in activities that strengthen their communities and the nation.

Why These Values Matter

Australian values are not just theoretical concepts; they are lived experiences that shape the nation's identity. They provide a framework for individuals to contribute meaningfully to society while enjoying the freedoms and opportunities that Australia offers. By explicitly teaching these values, particularly to migrants and the younger generation, Australia can ensure that its cultural legacy continues to thrive while adapting to an increasingly globalised world.

These values are also a significant reason why so many people aspire to become Australian citizens. They represent a vision of a society that is fair, free, inclusive, and supportive - a society where everyone can find a place to belong. By embracing and teaching these values, Australia strengthens its foundations and builds a brighter, more cohesive future for all.

Mandatory Cultural Orientation: New migrants should undergo programs that include lessons on Australian values, legal rights, and responsibilities. This not only aids integration but also reduces cultural tensions.

Linking *Life. Be in it.* to Australian Values
The *Life. Be in it.* campaign aligns seamlessly with Australia's core values, including mateship, larrikin spirit, and community participation. Its emphasis on getting Australians to engage in active lifestyles transcends mere physical health, promoting inclusivity by encouraging people from diverse backgrounds to come together in sports, recreation, and shared community activities.

As Dr. Benjamin observed, culture acts as a "cushion," providing people with a sense of belonging and resilience against life's challenges. Initiatives like *Life. Be in it.* demonstrate how cultural frameworks, underpinned by humour, relatability, and accessibility, can empower individuals to take control of their lives. This empowerment, in turn, reinforces the social fabric, promoting both personal well-being and societal cohesion.

SEWA - Serving Eternally Without Acknowledgement (Singh 2024).
The Sikh concept of *Sewa*, or selfless service, provides a powerful framework for inspiring purpose-driven individuals who contribute meaningfully to the collective well-being of society. *Sewa* transcends mere charity; it embodies the principle of serving without expectation, motivated purely by compassion and a sense of duty toward one's community. Rooted in the belief that all of humanity is interconnected, *Sewa* instils a profound sense of responsibility for one's neighbours and the broader society. By engaging in acts of service - whether through feeding the hungry, supporting those in crisis, or advocating for social justice - individuals practicing *Sewa* create a ripple effect of positivity and inclusion.

In the context of Cultural Education, incorporating the ethos of *Sewa* encourages students, employees, and community members to adopt a service-oriented mindset. It not only strengthens societal bonds but also builds environments of psychological safety, where mutual care and respect are paramount. By embedding *Sewa* into educational and corporate practices, we can inspire individuals to contribute toward a collective vision of harmony and progress, reinforcing the value of selflessness in building inclusive and resilient communities.

Values-based education begins at home, and its impact can resonate far beyond the confines of the family unit. A personal anecdote underscores this principle. My daughter, Saahiel, was once posed a thought-provoking question by her Year 9 Social Science teacher: "If you were going to choose how you would like to die, how would you like to die?" The teacher, who had asked this question for over two decades to combat students' egos and prepare them for life's realities, was accustomed to hearing familiar responses like "in my sleep," "free of pain," or "surrounded by loved ones." When she reached Saahiel, the response was profoundly different: "If I were going to choose how I was going to die, I would like to die saving someone else."

The teacher later called me, astonished. She expressed her gratitude for how we had raised Saahiel, acknowledging that in all her years, she had never heard such a selfless answer. While she admitted knowing little about our faith, her gratitude underscored the importance of instilling values like compassion, sacrifice, and responsibility to others - principles that are central to the Sikh concept of *sewa* (selfless service).

This moment highlights how values imparted at home can shape a young person's character and worldview. It underscores the role of Cultural Education in nurturing future generations who are not only aware of themselves but also deeply committed to the well-being of others.

Respectful Relationships: Foundations for Psychological Safety

"Respectful Relationships" programs, increasingly adopted by Australian states, aim to embed the principles of respect, empathy, and equity into school curricula. These programs address issues like gender equality, consent, bullying, and conflict resolution, equipping students with the tools to build healthy relationships. They also create environments where psychological safety is a priority, encouraging open dialogue and mutual respect among peers.

Core Components of Respectful Relationships

1. **Consent Education:** Teaching the importance of informed, voluntary, and enthusiastic agreement in all interpersonal interactions. This builds a foundation for mutual respect and understanding in relationships.

2. **Gender Equality:** Addressing biases and stereotypes early to challenge harmful norms, ensuring students grow into adults who respect and value diversity.

3. **Bullying Prevention:** Providing students with strategies to recognise, address, and prevent bullying, creating a culture of accountability and empathy.

4. **Conflict Resolution:** Teaching skills for managing disagreements constructively, which is

crucial for psychological safety and long-term relationship-building.

Best Practices for Implementation

To maximize the effectiveness of "Respectful Relationships," best practices should be adopted across all layers of society:

1. **Whole-School Approach:** Schools should involve teachers, students, and parents, ensuring the program's principles are reflected in school policies, teaching practices, and the broader school culture.

2. **Culturally Inclusive Content:** Materials must be designed to reflect the diversity of Australian society, ensuring they resonate with students from varied cultural backgrounds. For instance, integrating narratives that respect CALD communities can reinforce the universal application of respect and equity.

3. **Teacher Training:** Educators must receive comprehensive training to deliver these programs effectively, ensuring sensitivity when addressing complex topics like consent, gender dynamics, and cultural diversity.

4. **Community Engagement:** Beyond the classroom, communities should be engaged through workshops, public campaigns, and partnerships with local organisations to reinforce these values at home and in public life.

5. **Monitoring and Feedback:** Schools should evaluate program outcomes through regular assessments, adjusting content and delivery

methods based on student feedback and societal changes.

Extending Respectful Relationships Beyond Schools

The principles of "Respectful Relationships" can extend to workplaces and community settings. For example, corporate diversity and inclusion programs can benefit from similar frameworks, addressing workplace harassment, unconscious bias, and inequity. Community workshops, supported by local governments, can help integrate these principles into everyday interactions.

Why This Matters

Respectful relationships are the bedrock of psychological safety. When individuals feel respected and valued, they are more likely to thrive, contribute meaningfully, and uphold harmony in their communities. Implementing these programs effectively ensures that students grow up understanding the importance of empathy, accountability, and equity - essential skills for navigating Australia's diverse society.

The Significance of Purpose in Life

Purpose, a driving force behind human behaviour, is critical for shaping a positive outlook on life and achieving personal and societal fulfilment. Research indicates that individuals with a clear sense of purpose tend to experience higher levels of motivation, improved mental health, and greater resilience when facing life's challenges (Hill and Turiano 2014). Purpose is not merely about achieving individual goals; it also involves contributing to something larger than oneself - be it family, community, or society.

In Australia, purpose-driven living aligns with the national value of resilience, which reflects the country's optimistic and determined spirit. Australians take pride in overcoming adversity, whether through acts of mateship during natural disasters or by lending a hand to neighbours in need Embedding purpose-driven education into cultural frameworks and workplaces can help instil this value, generating a sense of shared responsibility and collective growth.

Practical Strategies for Purpose Development
1. **Goal Setting**: Research shows that goal setting is a powerful mechanism for cultivating purpose. Clear, achievable objectives help individuals focus their energy, track progress, and celebrate milestones (Locke & Latham 2015). Programs within schools, workplaces, and community organisations can teach structured goal-setting techniques to instil a sense of purpose from an early age.

2. **Fulfilment Through Contribution**: Evidence from Cultural Education initiatives suggests that engaging in community service, such as *sewa* (selfless service), enhances personal fulfilment and cultivates empathy. Purpose-driven programs should encourage individuals to explore how their unique strengths can positively impact society, creating a feedback loop of personal growth and societal benefit.

3. **Emphasising Growth Over Achievement**: A purpose-driven lifestyle is not just about reaching a final destination. It is about valuing the journey. This ties directly to Australia's egalitarian values, encouraging individuals to find purpose in

personal development, lifelong learning, and forming meaningful connections with others.

Purpose as a Cultural Value

Australians are known for their optimistic, 'glass-half-full' outlook on life, an attitude that is intrinsically tied to the notion of purpose. Mateship, a cornerstone of Australian values, embodies the idea of finding purpose in supporting one another. Encouraging purpose-driven living reinforces this spirit, ensuring that individuals not only find meaning in their personal lives but also contribute to building inclusive, cohesive communities.

Embedding purpose-driven education into school curricula, community programs, and workplace initiatives can have profound effects. For instance, teaching young people the value of setting and achieving goals, while instilling resilience and optimism, can help combat mental health challenges. For adults, purpose-driven frameworks in workplaces can enhance employee engagement, productivity, and overall satisfaction.

Research-Based Impact of Purpose

Studies by researchers like George and Park (2016), highlight that individuals with a strong sense of purpose exhibit:

- Lower rates of anxiety and depression.
- Increased motivation and job satisfaction.
- Greater social connectedness and community involvement.

Globally, countries that integrate purpose-driven education and societal frameworks, such as Finland's emphasis on holistic well-being in schools, demonstrate higher levels of happiness and societal cohesion.

'Reverse Migration': A Consequence of Workplace Discrimination

Australia's skilled migration program has attracted a diverse and talented workforce, with permanent migrants comprising 26.3% of all jobs in the country as of 2019-20. Notably, 59% of the 3 million permanent migrants who arrived since 2000 entered through the skilled stream, equating to approximately 1.76 million individuals (ABS 2024). Despite their qualifications and contributions, many of these skilled migrants encounter systemic barriers that hinder their career progression. Biases, stereotypes, and a lack of cultural competence within corporate and government sectors often result in limited access to senior positions, leading to frustration and disillusionment.

This systemic discrimination not only affects the psychological safety of migrant employees but also prompts a troubling trend of reverse migration as mentioned in the previous chapter. Skilled professionals, after investing years in Australia, are choosing to return to their countries of origin, where they perceive better career opportunities and a more inclusive environment. This exodus represents a significant loss of talent and expertise for Australia, undermining the objectives of its skilled migration policies.

Addressing this issue requires a concerted effort to shape inclusive workplace cultures that value diversity and provide equitable opportunities for advancement. Implementing comprehensive Cultural Education programs can help dismantle biases and create environments where all employees feel respected and empowered. By prioritising psychological safety and inclusivity, Australian organisations can retain their skilled migrant workforce, thereby enhancing innovation and maintaining economic competitiveness.

In summary, 'reverse migration' serves as a critical indicator of the need for systemic change within Australian workplaces. By addressing the underlying causes of discrimination and promoting inclusive cultures, Australia can mitigate this trend and fully leverage the potential of its diverse talent pool.

Visualisation: Harnessing the Power of the Mind

Visualisation is the mental practice of imagining desired outcomes as a means to achieving them. It is a technique rooted in both psychological and cultural traditions, with research and anecdotes demonstrating its profound impact on goal attainment, motivation, and mental resilience. Visualisation transcends mere daydreaming; it involves focusing on clear, actionable goals while aligning mental and emotional energy towards achieving them.

The Science of Visualisation

Studies in neuroscience have revealed that visualising success activates the same neural pathways as actually experiencing it. This phenomenon, often referred to as "mental rehearsal," strengthens the brains capacity to perform associated actions, effectively priming individuals for success (Driskell et al. 1994). Athletes, entrepreneurs, and artists have long used visualisation to prepare for high-pressure situations, improve performance, and overcome self-doubt. According to research by Taylor et al. (1998), individuals who use visualisation for goal-setting and problem-solving are more likely to achieve their objectives compared to those who rely solely on traditional methods.

A Real-Life Example: Michael Jackson's Concert

When my youngest sister Parvyn was nine, she was a huge Michael Jackson fan and desperately wanted to attend his 'History Down Under' tour. However, due to financial constraints purchasing tickets seemed impossible. Despite the odds, my father visualised all three of us attending the concert together. Each day, as he walked along Brighton Beach (in Adelaide where we grew up), he mentally pictured us at the event. While visualisation alone didn't magically produce tickets, the alignment of belief, effort, and the eventual opportunity provided by a children's advocacy organisation we had performed for at their charity event, led not only to us attending but to an unforgettable experience. We not only met Michael Jackson but also sang with him on stage. This incredible chain of events underscores the power of mental focus combined with action.

Visualisation in Cultural Education

Visualisation has been deeply embedded in various cultural and spiritual practices worldwide. From guided imagery in mindfulness exercises to traditional storytelling that evokes aspirational thinking, the act of imagining positive futures is universal. Integrating visualisation exercises into educational frameworks as part of Cultural Education can equip individuals with a powerful tool for navigating challenges, setting goals, and finding purpose.

For example:
- **In schools**: Students could use visualisation techniques for academic success, imagining themselves mastering difficult concepts or excelling in projects.

- **In workplaces**: Employees can use it to overcome professional challenges or achieve career milestones, promoting productivity and satisfaction.

- **In community programs**: Visualisation can be used to advance social cohesion by encouraging participants to imagine shared goals, such as peaceful communities or environmental sustainability.

Beyond Placebo: The Real Impact of Visualisation

While some might dismiss visualisation as merely a placebo, research consistently supports its effectiveness. A study by Wager and Atlas (2015) showed that participants who visualised achieving their goals demonstrated higher resilience and self-discipline. Moreover, cultural traditions that emphasise visualisation, such as Tibetan Buddhist practices or Indigenous dreaming ceremonies, demonstrate its role in contributing to personal and collective growth.

The Role of Visualisation in Cultural Education Frameworks

Visualisation should be recognised as a practical tool within the Cultural Education framework, empowering individuals to dream big, stay motivated, and overcome perceived barriers. Whether applied to personal development, professional settings, or advancing societal inclusivity, visualisation offers a way to inspire action and generate hope.

Mindfulness: A Foundation for Psychological Safety and Resilience

Mindfulness, the practice of being fully present and aware of the moment without judgment, has emerged as a powerful tool for developing psychological safety and emotional resilience. Originating from ancient traditions, particularly Buddhism, mindfulness is now a cornerstone of modern mental health and well-being strategies, validated by extensive research.

The Role of Mindfulness in Education and Workplaces

Jon Kabat-Zinn, the pioneer of mindfulness-based stress reduction (MBSR), demonstrated that regular mindfulness practice reduces symptoms of anxiety and depression, enhances emotional regulation, and improves cognitive functioning (Kabat-Zinn 2003). Schools and workplaces incorporating mindfulness have seen measurable benefits. Studies in education, such as those by Schonert-Reichl (2023), reveal that mindfulness programs enhance empathy, classroom behaviour, and student focus. Similarly, workplaces employing mindfulness initiatives report higher employee satisfaction, reduced burnout, and improved productivity.

An illustrative example comes from a school workshop in South Australia. A simple breathing exercise was introduced, teaching students to focus on deep breaths by placing one hand on their chest and the other on their belly. Weeks later, a principal shared the transformative impact this had on a previously disruptive Year 4 student. The child, instead of reacting with frustration, practised the technique to calm himself, resulting in a dramatic improvement in his behaviour and focus.

Embedding mindfulness into Cultural Education equips individuals with tools to navigate stress and emotional turbulence, harnessing resilience and empathy - critical components for creating inclusive and harmonious societies.

Avoiding the Pitfalls of Misaligned Initiatives

While mindfulness can be transformative, poorly aligned Cultural Education initiatives risk undermining psychological safety. A case in point involved a Sudanese artist invited to a primary school to conduct a cultural workshop. While his drum and dance activities captivated Year 2 students, his recounting of personal war experiences was emotionally intense and inappropriate for the audience's developmental stage. The result was confusion, anxiety, and distress among the children, overshadowing the positive aspects of the session.

Such examples underscore the importance of tailoring initiatives to their audience. Facilitators must receive specialised training to ensure content delivery is age-appropriate, culturally sensitive, and aligned with the program's objectives. Additionally, resilience-building components should accompany challenging topics to help participants process and contextualise information constructively.

Implications for Businesses

Misalignment is not limited to educational settings; it also impacts organizations. According to a Deloitte report (2022), 56% of employees in workplaces with poorly executed diversity and inclusion programs reported feeling disengaged, compared to 25% in organisations with effective training. Moreover, superficial or "performative" initiatives damage reputations and erode trust among customers and stakeholders. Effective mindfulness and Cultural Education programs can enhance team cohesion, inspire innovation, and build genuine inclusivity, ultimately benefiting both the workforce and the organization's bottom line.

A Holistic Approach

Incorporating mindfulness into the broader framework of Cultural Education strengthens its impact across societal sectors. By equipping individuals with strategies to manage stress, practice empathy, and navigate diverse environments, mindfulness contributes to psychological safety and resilience. This integration ensures that Cultural Education fulfills its promise—not merely as an academic exercise but as a transformative force for inclusivity, emotional well-being, and societal harmony.

Measuring Impact: Longitudinal Studies and Success Stories

Evaluating the effectiveness of early education interventions is critical for refining strategies, demonstrating their value, and ensuring long-term positive outcomes for individuals and communities.

Longitudinal Studies
The Roots of Empathy Program (Canada)

The Roots of Empathy program, a widely recognised initiative from Canada, fosters emotional intelligence and social empathy in school-aged children. Central to the program is the involvement of infants - along with their parents or caregivers - who visit classrooms over the course of a school year. Guided by trained facilitators, students observe and discuss the infants' behaviours, emotions, and development. Through these interactions, children are encouraged to reflect on their own feelings and the feelings of others, building their capacity for empathy.

Research spanning over two decades demonstrates the program's long-term impact. Participants consistently report lower levels of aggression and bullying behaviour, along with an increased tendency toward inclusive and

133

prosocial actions as they mature (Roots of Empathy 2021). This method emphasises that cultivating empathy at a young age can have ripple effects across a child's interactions and decisions well into adulthood.

Diversity Education in Sweden
Sweden's education policies prioritise teaching respect for cultural diversity, beginning in early childhood and continuing through secondary school. These policies include immersive social studies programs, interactive activities, and multicultural content in curricula, aiming to normalise diversity and build mutual respect amongst students from different backgrounds.
Longitudinal research conducted by the Swedish Ministry of Education tracked students exposed to these diversity education programs. Findings revealed that participants were more likely to demonstrate tolerance, social responsibility, and civic engagement in adulthood compared to those who had not been part of similar initiatives (SME 2022). These results underline the importance of sustained, intentional cultural education in shaping attitudes and behaviours over time.

Success Stories
- **Australian Schools**
  Schools participating in the Harmony Day initiative have reported increased cultural awareness and reduced instances of bullying among students. This program, which celebrates Australia's multicultural heritage, exemplifies how education can bridge divides and foster unity (DOE 2022).

Opportunities and Challenges
Despite the successes of early education interventions, challenges remain.

Opportunities

- **Global Collaboration:** Sharing best practices across nations can enhance Cultural Education programs.

- **Technology Integration:** Digital tools, such as virtual reality and online cultural exchanges, can make learning more engaging and accessible. Tools like 'Diversity Atlas' by Cultural Infusion led by Peter Mousaferiadis (Cultural Infusion 2024).

Challenges

- **Resource Disparities:** Schools in underfunded regions may struggle to implement comprehensive Cultural Education programs.

- **Resistance to Change:** Societal and political resistance can hinder the adoption of inclusive curricula.

Global Perspectives on Cultural Education and Psychological Safety

Learning from international models provides actionable insights for Australia.

New Zealand: Te Ao Māori and Bicultural Education

New Zealand's bicultural approach to education reflects its commitment to the Treaty of Waitangi, ensuring Māori perspectives are integrated into the curriculum. The Te Ao Māori framework teaches all students the language, customs, and values of New Zealand's Indigenous population. This initiative has significantly increased cultural awareness among non-Māori students while instilling pride in Māori heritage. And of course the

Hakka as a precursor to any international game involving New Zealanders send chills not only amoungst the opposition but the entire stadium.

New Zealand's police force is a case study in applying cultural competency to public service. Officers undergo cultural training that teaches them how to engage respectfully with Māori and Pasifika communities, resulting in reduced tensions and increased trust (NZME 2023).

Singapore: Balancing Multiracial Harmony with Underlying Pressures

Singapore is globally recognised as a model of multiracial harmony, driven by a deliberate government-led approach to integration. Policies such as the Ethnic Integration Policy ensure a balanced distribution of ethnic groups within public housing estates, enabling everyday interactions across racial lines. The national curriculum includes mandatory Mother Tongue Languages to preserve cultural roots, while public campaigns like *Racial Harmony Day* emphasise respect and understanding among its citizens.

However, beneath this structured harmony lie significant societal pressures, which have contributed to Singapore's relatively high suicide rates, particularly among youth and the elderly. The juxtaposition of enforced harmony and personal struggles reveals complexities in managing cultural integration while safeguarding mental well-being.

Factors Contributing to Singapore's Suicide Rates
High Academic and Social Expectations
- Singapore's education system is renowned for its academic rigour, but it also places immense

pressure on students. From a young age, children are subjected to competitive examinations and streaming systems that determine future opportunities. This intense focus on academic performance can lead to stress, anxiety, and feelings of inadequacy.

- According to the Samaritans of Singapore (SOS 2021), suicide remains the leading cause of death for individuals aged 10–29. In 2020 alone, 452 suicide deaths were recorded, marking a worrying trend in a society striving for excellence.

Elderly Loneliness and Societal Shifts

- Singapore's rapidly aging population faces issues of loneliness and neglect. As younger generations focus on career demands and nuclear family structures, many elderly individuals feel isolated. The erosion of traditional extended family support systems exacerbates this problem, leading to mental health struggles among the senior demographic.

Economic Pressures

- While Singapore enjoys one of the highest GDP per capita rates globally, economic inequality remains a challenge. Rising living costs and the need to maintain a high standard of living contribute to financial stress among middle and lower-income families.
- Immigrant workers, who play a critical role in Singapore's economic success, often face challenging conditions, including discrimination, low wages, and social isolation, leading to vulnerabilities in mental health.

Stigma Around Mental Health

- Despite advancements, mental health stigma persists in Singapore. Many individuals are reluctant to seek help due to societal perceptions of weakness or failure, particularly in a culture that values resilience and achievement.
- According to the Singapore Mental Health Study, nearly one in seven Singaporeans experienced a mental health condition in their lifetime, yet less than one-quarter sought professional help.

Lessons for Cultural Education and Policy

The Singaporean experience underscores the importance of addressing the hidden costs of a meritocratic and harmonious society. While Cultural Education plays a pivotal role in strengthening unity, it must also include a focus on mental health awareness, self-acceptance, and reducing societal pressures. Policymakers and educators can take the following steps:

1. **Integrating Mental Health Education into Cultural Education**
   - Introduce programs that teach students and workers the importance of mental well-being alongside cultural appreciation. This could involve visualisation / mindfulness exercises, stress management workshops, and open discussions about mental health issues.

2. **Creating Safe Spaces for Expression**
   - Schools, workplaces, and community centres should provide safe spaces where individuals can discuss their challenges without fear of judgment. These spaces would help bridge the gap between societal expectations and individual struggles.

3. **Encouraging a Shift in Societal Values**
   o Move beyond defining success purely through academic or financial achievements. Recognise diverse paths to fulfilment, including the arts, volunteerism, and community service, as equally valuable contributions to society.

4. **Fostering Intergenerational Bonds**
   o Develop initiatives that bring together younger and older generations to share experiences and stories. Cultural Education can play a role in reminding individuals of the importance of familial and community ties, which are crucial in reducing isolation among the elderly.

5. **Continuous Improvement Cultural Responsiveness Tools**
   o CICRT offers a valuable example of embedding cultural responsiveness in social work education, suggesting that similar tools could be developed for broader application across industries and sectors (CICRT 2024).

South Africa: Addressing Historical Divisions

In South Africa, Cultural Education is an essential tool for healing the wounds of apartheid. The *Revised National Curriculum Statement* incorporates lessons on human rights, diversity, and anti-discrimination from early childhood. Schools are encouraged to celebrate national heritage days, where students learn about each others languages, cuisine, and customs.

Corporate initiatives such as those by Discovery Limited, a leading financial services company, have embraced cultural competency training to promote inclusivity. The company's programs address racial and cultural dynamics in the workplace, leading to increased employee engagement and reduced instances of discrimination (Acemoglu et al. 2007).

Germany: Cultural Education for Integration

Germany's approach to Cultural Education focuses heavily on integrating migrants and refugees. Since the influx of refugees in 2015, the government has implemented mandatory *Integration Courses* that combine German language lessons with cultural orientation. These courses cover topics like democracy, gender equality, and social norms, helping newcomers adapt while promoting societal acceptance.

German schools also offer intercultural training to teachers, ensuring that they can address the needs of students from diverse backgrounds. While successful in many respects, Germany continues to grapple with challenges such as rising xenophobia and uneven regional implementation of integration policies (GFOMR 2023).

United States: A Fragmented Approach to Cultural Education

The United States presents a complex and often contradictory case for Cultural Education, reflecting its vast diversity and deep societal divides. As a melting pot of cultures, ethnicities, and beliefs, the U.S. has long grappled with integrating diverse groups while addressing systemic inequities. The nation's approach to Cultural Education is heavily influenced by its decentralised education system, political polarisation, and evolving societal dynamics. This can often lead to ghetto mentalities amongst some ethnic groups.

Cultural Education in Schools
In the U.S., Cultural Education initiatives vary significantly by state and district due to the decentralised nature of the education system. While some states have implemented comprehensive diversity and inclusion curricula, others have resisted, citing concerns about indoctrination or cultural biases. Controversial debates over Critical Race Theory (CRT) exemplify the fragmented approach, with proponents arguing for a deeper understanding of systemic racism and critics claiming it promotes divisiveness.

A Pew Research Center survey (2022) highlighted these divisions:
- 44% of Americans believed that increased discussions of racism and racial inequality in schools were a good thing, while 34% thought they were bad for society.
- Support for culturally inclusive curricula was highest among younger adults (61%) and racial minorities (71%), compared to older adults and white respondents.

Political Polarisation and Leadership Influence
The elections of Donald Trump (2016) and Kamala Harris (as Vice President in 2020) reveal stark contrasts in how cultural identity shapes American politics and policy preferences.

Donald Trump and the Politics of Nationalism
- Trump's presidency often amplified nationalist rhetoric, appealing to a base that viewed multiculturalism as a threat to traditional American values. His administration rolled back

diversity training in federal agencies, claiming it was "divisive" and "un-American."

- Under Trump's leadership, the "America First" policy became a rallying cry for those who felt left behind by globalisation and multiculturalism. However, this rhetoric also deepened societal divides, as seen in the rise of hate crimes during his presidency. The FBI reported a 12% increase in hate crimes in 2019, with the majority targeting racial and ethnic minorities.

Kamala Harris and the Politics of Representation
- The election of Kamala Harris as the first female Vice President of African and South Asian descent marked a significant moment in U.S. history. Her representation was celebrated as a victory for cultural diversity and inclusion, particularly among immigrant communities and younger generations.

- Harris's visibility has inspired discussions about cultural competency in governance, with her background emphasising the importance of embracing multifaceted identities. A 2021 YouGov poll revealed that 56% of Americans viewed her election as a step forward for diversity in leadership, compared to 28% who saw it as insignificant.

Public Sentiments on Cultural Education in USA
Polling data suggests that Americans value Cultural Education but remain divided on its implementation:
- A 2022 survey by Education Week found that 72% of educators supported incorporating multicultural perspectives into teaching, while 48% of parents

expressed concerns about these initiatives overshadowing traditional curricula.

- In contrast, younger Americans overwhelmingly favour Cultural Education. A 2023 Pew study indicated that 67% of Gen Z adults believe schools should do more to teach diversity and inclusion, compared to 38% of Baby Boomers.

Barriers to Effective Cultural Education in USA
1. Political and Social Fragmentation
- States like California and New York have embraced Cultural Education through ethnic studies mandates and bilingual programs. However, states in the South and Midwest often resist such efforts, reflecting the broader political divide.

- This fragmentation creates inequities in access to Cultural Education, leaving students in certain regions without exposure to diverse perspectives.

2. Media and Misinformation
- Media outlets often fuel division by framing Cultural Education debates as zero-sum conflicts, where one group's gain is perceived as another's loss. This exacerbates polarisation and undermines efforts to build consensus on the benefits of cultural awareness.

What Americans Want
Despite political divides, many Americans recognise the need for cultural competency:

- According to a 2020 Gallup poll, 71% of respondents agreed that understanding diverse perspectives is critical to preparing students for the future workforce.

- However, the same survey found that only 34% believed schools were adequately addressing cultural diversity, highlighting a gap between public expectations and current practices.

Lessons for the Future

The United States' experience underscores the importance of bipartisan efforts to implement Cultural Education. Policies that transcend political divides and emphasise shared values - such as equality, freedom, and opportunity - can build a more inclusive society.

Collaborative approaches, like partnerships between schools, community organisations, and corporations, are essential to bridging gaps and building consensus.

As the U.S. navigates its cultural and political challenges, investing in education that promotes empathy, critical thinking, and civic engagement remains paramount. By prioritising Cultural Education, the nation can move toward a more united and resilient future.

The 2024 U.S. presidential election, culminating in Donald Trump's victory over Kamala Harris, underscored the nation's deep divisions on Cultural Education and related policies. Trump's campaign emphasised a return to traditional American values, advocating for the elimination of the Department of Education and the promotion of "patriotic" education. He appointed Linda McMahon to lead these efforts, signalling a shift toward state-controlled education systems and curricula that emphasise national pride (Charter 2024).

Conversely, Harris's platform focused on diversity and inclusion, aiming to integrate comprehensive Cultural

Education into schools to reflect America's multicultural fabric. Despite her efforts, the election results indicated a preference amongst voters for Trump's vision, suggesting a desire for educational reforms that prioritise traditional narratives over multicultural perspectives.

This electoral outcome highlights the fragmented approach to Cultural Education in the United States, with significant disparities in how states and communities address diversity in their curricula. The contrasting platforms of Trump and Harris reflect the broader national debate on the role of Cultural Education in shaping societal values and identity.

Moving forward, it is crucial for policymakers and educators to navigate these divisions thoughtfully, striving to create educational environments that honour the nation's diverse heritage while solidifying unity and mutual respect.

Tackling Hard Truths
Creating psychologically safe environments requires confronting uncomfortable realities.

1. Addressing Ghetto Mentality
Clusters of migrant communities can create insular environments that hinder integration.
- **The Somali Community in Melbourne:** Reports highlight high unemployment rates, crime rates and limited interaction with broader Australian society. Initiatives like mentorship programs and language classes are essential to breaking down barriers.

2. Promoting Language Proficiency

English proficiency is critical for social and economic integration. However, enforcing language acquisition must be done sensitively.

Opportunities for Action

Cultural Education must evolve beyond theory into actionable frameworks.

1. Policymaker Accountability

Legislators must ensure cultural competency in policy development.

- Representation in Parliament: Australia's Parliament remains disproportionately Anglo-Saxon. Increasing representation from diverse backgrounds will ensure more inclusive policymaking.

2. Corporate Initiatives

Businesses must embrace Cultural Education as part of their corporate social responsibility.

- **Diversity Audits / Cultural Workplace Reviews:** Regular assessments of workplace diversity and inclusion practices can identify gaps and guide improvements.

3. Community-Led Solutions

Grassroots initiatives must lead the charge in bridging divides.

- Example: Interfaith dialogues and shared cultural events promote understanding and break down barriers.

Conclusion: The Path Forward

Cultural Education is a transformative tool for creating psychologically safe environments. By addressing biases, facilitating inclusivity, and equipping individuals with cultural competencies, societies can unlock their full potential.

Australia must draw lessons from global successes and failures, tailoring its policies and practices to its unique multicultural landscape. Psychological safety is not a luxury but a necessity for innovation, cohesion, and progress. Through intentional action and unwavering commitment, we can build a society where every individual feels valued, respected, and empowered to thrive.

Chapter 8
Toward a Global Framework for Cultural Responsiveness

As societies grow increasingly interconnected, the need for a cohesive and adaptable global framework for cultural responsiveness has never been more urgent. This chapter delves into international models, grassroots issues, and forward-thinking policies that inform the development of a comprehensive, data-driven strategy for global Cultural Education.

Comparative Analysis of Cultural Education Models

Finland: Equitable Education and Cultural Sensitivity

Finland's education system is globally recognised for its emphasis on equity and inclusivity. Cultural Education is woven into its core curriculum through *National Core Curricula for Basic Education*. This includes ethics, history, and arts education that celebrate Finland's Sami Indigenous population and immigrant communities.

Data shows that Finnish students consistently score high on global happiness and well-being indices. Surveys by the Organisation for Economic Co-operation and Development indicate that Finnish students experience significantly lower levels of bullying and discrimination compared to peers in other countries, attributed to the system's inclusivity-focused policies (FNAE 2021).

United Arab Emirates (UAE): Mandating Cultural Tolerance

The UAE launched its *National Tolerance Program* in 2016, emphasising tolerance and Cultural Education as pillars of societal development. The government mandated cultural competency training for public sector employees, with schools incorporating lessons on coexistence and respect for all faiths and nationalities.

Despite the UAE's success in developing a diverse expatriate community, it faces criticism for uneven application of tolerance laws. However, its cultural initiatives have contributed to increased satisfaction among expatriates, with 78% reporting improved feelings of safety and belonging (UAE 2024).

In discussing tolerance within the context of the United Arab Emirates' legislated cultural tolerance framework, it is essential to scrutinise the very concept of "tolerance." The dictionary defines tolerance as "the ability or willingness to tolerate the existence of opinions or behaviour that one dislikes or disagrees with" (Oxford 2024). This implies enduring or 'putting up with' something, rather than fully accepting or embracing it. To tolerate brussel sprouts at the dinner table, for instance, does not mean one enjoys or values them - it merely means one endures their presence. Applying this framework to human relationships raises profound questions: should we merely 'put up with' our fellow human beings, or should we strive for acceptance, understanding, and respect?

Legislation around tolerance, such as that in the UAE, sends an important signal about the need for coexistence in diverse societies. However, framing the concept within the language of tolerance may inadvertently imply begrudging acceptance rather than encouraging genuine inclusion or celebration of diversity. For societies to truly flourish, policies and Cultural Education should aspire to move beyond tolerance, cultivating environments where individuals feel respected, valued, and empowered to express their identities.

As someone who believes in the principle of "you do you, but leave me to do me," the idea of legislating tolerance feels insufficient. It sets a low bar for societal harmony. Instead of aspiring merely to tolerate each other, we should aim to create systems that promote understanding, empathy, and acceptance - pillars upon which inclusivity and equity are truly built. By doing so, we move away from the passive act of tolerance toward the active engagement with our shared humanity.

Brazil: Bridging Cultural Divides through Afro-Brazilian Studies

Brazilian education law mandates the teaching of Afro-Brazilian and Indigenous history and culture in schools. This policy aims to combat the pervasive racial inequality rooted in Brazil's colonial past. The curriculum incorporates topics such as African heritage, Indigenous languages, and the legacy of slavery.

While the law represents a progressive step, implementation has been inconsistent. A 2021 survey by the Brazilian Institute for Geography and Statistics revealed that only 40% of schools fully adopted the mandated curriculum (OECD 2021). Nonetheless, where implemented effectively, schools report higher levels of cross-racial understanding among students.

Kenya: Rebuilding After Conflict

Kenya's *National Cohesion and Integration Commission* focuses on promoting interethnic harmony following decades of political and ethnic conflict. Cultural Education initiatives in schools encourage dialogue between students from different ethnic groups, emphasising shared history and common values.

A 2022 study by the African Centre for Peace and Conflict Studies found that students participating in cultural dialogue programs were 45% less likely to exhibit bias against other ethnic groups than their peers (CPCS 2022).

Lessons Learned: Grassroots Issues and Global Challenges

Grassroots Issues in Cultural Responsiveness

Grassroots issues often serve as barriers to the success of Cultural Education programs. These include:

1. **Language Barriers:** Multilingual societies like South Africa struggle to balance the preservation of native languages with the practicalities of teaching in a unifying language like English.
2. **Economic Disparities:** Countries with underfunded education systems, such as India, face challenges in implementing nationwide Cultural Education policies (Hillman and Jenker 2004).
3. **Resistance to Change:** Conservative societies often view Cultural Education initiatives as threats to traditional values.

Global Challenges

1. **Polarisation:** Rising nationalism in countries such as Hungary and the U.S. has hindered efforts to promote cultural inclusion.

2. **Digital Misinformation:** The spread of misinformation on social media has exacerbated cultural divides globally. For instance, false narratives about migration have led to increased xenophobia in parts of Europe (ECARI 2021).
3. **Policy Inconsistencies:** Even countries with progressive policies, such as Canada, face challenges in uniformly applying Cultural Education across diverse regions.

Proposing a Global Framework for Cultural Responsiveness

Core Principles
1. **Respect for Diversity:** Recognising and celebrating differences rather than tolerating them.
2. **Empathy and Understanding:** Training educators, policymakers, and corporate leaders to prioritise emotional intelligence.
3. **Inclusive Narratives:** Promoting stories that highlight shared human experiences across cultures.

Adaptability to Local Contexts
1. **Community-Centric Policies:** Policies must be tailored to reflect the unique cultural dynamics of each society. For instance, Australia's focus on reconciliation with First Nations people could serve as a model for other countries grappling with colonial legacies.
2. **Flexible Curriculum Design:** Curricula should include mandatory Cultural Education components while allowing schools to adapt lessons to local needs.

Leveraging Technology
1. **Global Exchange Programs:** Platforms like eTwinning enable students and teachers from different countries to collaborate on cultural projects.
2. **AI-Powered Training:** AI tools like Diversity Atlas, can provide personalised cultural competency training for individuals in public service and corporate roles.

Case Studies: Success Stories and Opportunities

Norway: Cultural Education and Refugee Integration

Norway has successfully integrated refugee children into its education system through targeted Cultural Education programs. Schools use interactive storytelling and theatre to teach Norwegian language and culture while celebrating the heritage of refugee students. As a result, 85% of refugee children feel included in their schools within one year (Norwegian Ministries 2021)

Rwanda: Peace Education Post-Genocide

Rwanda's *National Unity and Reconciliation Commission* integrates Cultural Education into peace-building initiatives. The *Itorero ry'Igihugu* program teaches Rwandans of all ages about the values of unity and respect for diversity. These efforts have contributed to a 60% decrease in ethnic-based discrimination over the past two decades (Gierszewska and Sinning 2023).

Germany: Intercultural Competence in Policing

In response to criticism of racial profiling, Germany introduced mandatory intercultural training for police officers. These programs include simulations and workshops on cultural norms, aiming to reduce implicit bias. Surveys show a 25% improvement in community trust since the program's implementation (GFOMR 2023).

Toward a Collaborative Future

Developing a global framework for cultural responsiveness requires international cooperation. Organisations such as UNESCO and the Organisation for Economic Co-operation and Development (OECD) could spearhead initiatives to standardise best practices, create cross-border educational resources, and track progress through annual cultural cohesion indices.

Key Actions for Stakeholders

1. **Policymakers:** Establish policies that incentivise inclusive practices in education and business.
2. **Educators:** Ignite empathy and curiosity through experiential learning and value-based education practices.
3. **Corporations:** Implement DEI metrics linked to executive performance.

Conclusion: The Role of Australia

As a multicultural nation, Australia is uniquely positioned to lead global discussions on cultural responsiveness. By adopting a holistic approach that combines Cultural Education with policy reform, Australia can serve as a model for other countries navigating the complexities of diversity.

Chapter 9
Discipline and Consequences: Building a Responsible Society

Introduction

Discipline, often misunderstood as punitive measures, is a crucial aspect of teaching responsibility, self-regulation, and respect for societal norms. In contemporary Australian society, the shift away from traditional forms of discipline to more lenient approaches has sparked debate about whether children are adequately prepared to understand the consequences of their actions. This chapter explores global and local practices in teaching discipline, the role of parents and educators, and the potential long-term societal effects of failing to address this critical issue.

Global Perspectives on Discipline

In some countries, such as Malaysia, corporal punishment remains culturally accepted. For example, rattan canes (*"rotan"*) are used to discipline children in schools and tuition centres (as well as at home), a practice that aims to instil immediate obedience. Their school has a Disciplinary Master, that walks around the school with his *"rotan"*. However, research suggests that corporal punishment is associated with negative outcomes, including mental health challenges, reduced cognitive abilities, and increased aggression in adulthood (Gershoff 2016). While these practices persist in certain regions, they highlight the need to balance discipline with approaches that build intrinsic motivation, consequences training and self-regulation.

Discipline in the Australian Context

In Australia, corporal punishment is banned in schools and in homes, reflecting the country's commitment to protecting children's rights. However, this shift has left a gap in effective strategies to teach consequences, especially as child crime rates rise. A report by the Australian Institute of Criminology (Australian Government 2024) indicates that youth crime, including property offences and assaults, has seen a marked increase in recent years. Without structured discipline at home or in educational settings, children may lack the understanding of how their actions impact others, leading to a cycle of poor decision-making and antisocial behaviour.

Sporting Culture as a Tool for Teaching Discipline and Consequences

Sport plays a pivotal role in shaping young minds, teaching values that extend far beyond the playing field. My experience as a player, umpire, and coach with Netball Victoria has demonstrated how sport can be a powerful medium for instilling discipline and helping children understand the consequences of their actions. This is especially evident when working with girls from CALD communities, who often face unique challenges in developing confidence and self-respect.

Participation in sports such as netball teaches young people the importance of **following rules, respecting authority, and understanding the outcomes of their choices** - essential elements of discipline. For young CALD girls, this environment provides a structured and supportive setting to learn critical life skills, such as:

- **Accountability**: Players learn that their actions, whether on or off the court, impact their team's success, engendering a sense of responsibility.

- **Respect**: Interacting with teammates, coaches, and opponents emphasises the importance of mutual respect, regardless of cultural or personal differences.
- **Resilience**: Through wins and losses, players experience the real-life consequences of effort and perseverance, equipping them to handle challenges with grace.

Sport also reinforces commitment and loyalty, as players are expected to attend training sessions, participate in matches, and work collaboratively with their team. These lessons translate into a deeper understanding of fairness, dedication, and the value of hard work - qualities that are vital in both personal and professional spheres.

Beyond individual growth, the impact of sport extends to families and communities. For CALD families, seeing their daughters excel in a traditionally Australian sport like netball creates pride and a sense of belonging, while also breaking down cultural stereotypes. Moreover, programs run by organisations like Netball Victoria demonstrate how structured sporting initiatives can create pathways for young people to feel empowered and valued in society.

By incorporating sports into broader Cultural Education frameworks, we can use this dynamic tool to teach discipline and consequences in a way that is engaging, effective, and deeply impactful. In doing so, we reinforce the core values that underpin an inclusive and cohesive society.

The Role of Parents and Educators
Discipline begins at home. However, modern parenting styles often prioritise positive reinforcement without balancing it with accountability. In schools, teachers face

challenges in enforcing discipline due to restrictive policies, fear of backlash, and limited resources. Programs like restorative justice in schools, which focus on making amends rather than punitive measures, have shown promise but require broader implementation and support (Barton and Gonzales 2015).

Simple Ways to Teach Consequences

1. **Clear Rules and Expectations**: Setting clear, age-appropriate rules helps children understand boundaries. For example, schools could adopt behaviour contracts that outline expected conduct and consequences for violations.
2. **Restorative Practices**: When rules are broken, children should engage in restorative practices, such as apologising to affected parties or performing community service within the school environment.
3. **Natural Consequences**: Allowing children to face natural consequences for their actions can be a powerful teacher. For instance, if a student fails to complete homework, they might lose free time to finish it during breaks.
4. **Parental Responsibility**: Encouraging parents to actively participate in their child's discipline through programs like Positive Parenting Programs (Triple P) can nurture a collaborative approach.

Consequences of Lax Discipline
Failing to address discipline has ripple effects on society. Rising juvenile crime rates, increased rates of bullying, and antisocial behaviours are symptoms of a broader cultural shift away from teaching accountability. A study by the Australian Bureau of Statistics (2024) highlights that 70% of youth offenders had prior interactions with

the justice system, indicating a pattern of unchecked behaviours escalating over time.

The Psychological Aspect
Children who are not taught consequences often struggle with impulse control and empathy, leading to difficulties in social interactions and long-term relationships. Dr. Stuart Shanker's (2016) work on self-regulation emphasises the importance of teaching children how to manage emotions and behaviours rather than merely punishing them. Incorporating these principles into Cultural Education frameworks can create a generation that understands the balance between freedom and responsibility.

Recommendations for Policy and Practice
1. **Mandate Discipline Training for Educators**: Providing teachers with tools to manage classrooms effectively while remaining within legal and ethical guidelines.
2. **Parental Education Programs**: Offering accessible workshops on child development and discipline strategies.
3. **Youth Justice Reform**: Introducing programs that hold juveniles accountable while addressing underlying issues, such as trauma or socioeconomic factors.
4. **Community-Based Interventions**: Encouraging local mentorship programs that teach life skills, responsibility, and empathy.

Conclusion
Discipline is not about punishment; it is about teaching accountability, empathy, and self-control. By integrating structured approaches to discipline within homes, schools, and communities, Australia can build a society

that values respect, responsibility, and inclusivity. Addressing this issue proactively ensures that children grow into adults who contribute positively to society, breaking cycles of crime and antisocial behaviour.

Chapter 10

Charting the Future: Opportunities for Growth in Cultural Education Research and Implementation

Whilst this publication establishes a foundational understanding of Cultural Education and its transformative potential, it is evident that significant gaps remain in data, research, and practical implementation. This chapter identifies these areas, highlighting next steps and the critical role of collaboration across sectors to deepen the global impact of Cultural Education.

Data Gaps: Expanding the Evidence Base

There is a pressing need for more granular data to understand the nuanced effects of Cultural Education across various demographics.

For instance:

- **Bullying and Discrimination Statistics:** While existing studies link Cultural Education to reduced bullying, longitudinal data exploring the sustained impact of such interventions over decades is sparse. A report by United Nations Educational Scientific and Cultural Organisation (UNESCO 2023), indicated that 30% of students globally report being bullied for their cultural or religious identity. More precise metrics are needed to connect Cultural Education programs with tangible declines in these incidents.

- **Corporate Inclusivity Metrics:** While diversity improves business outcomes, there is insufficient data tracking how Cultural Education in corporate training programs affects long-term employee retention and satisfaction.

- **Geographic Comparisons:** Regional studies are necessary to compare the effectiveness of Cultural Education policies in rural versus urban settings, addressing unique challenges faced by these communities.

Collaboration Opportunities

The advancement of Cultural Education requires a coalition of diverse stakeholders, including governments, academic institutions, and grassroots organisations:

- **Educational Partnerships:** Universities and schools can partner to pilot innovative programs, such as integrating virtual reality (VR) technology to simulate immersive cultural experiences.
- **Corporate Collaborations:** Companies like Google and Commonwealth Bank, which have robust DEI initiatives, can collaborate with policymakers to design frameworks that link workplace inclusivity to national education strategies.
- **Community-Based Organisations:** Groups like Australia's Harmony Alliance and international bodies like the European Network Against Racism can offer ground-level insights to make policies more actionable.

Research Directions

Further exploration is required in the following areas:

1. **Mental Health Correlations:** Examining the link between Cultural Education and improved mental health outcomes, particularly in

communities experiencing systemic discrimination.

2. **Digital Tools and Platforms:** Investigating the efficacy of apps and online platforms in promoting cross-cultural understanding amongst younger generations.

3. **Unintended Consequences:** Analysing cases where Cultural Education has inadvertently reinforced stereotypes or created divisive narratives.

4. **Economic Impacts:** Expanding studies on how inclusive cultural policies contribute to national economic growth, such as increased tourism and foreign investment.

Case Studies for Inspiration

- **Singapore's Social Harmony Framework:** Singapore's government mandates cross-cultural interaction through housing policies and education. However, while these efforts are largely successful, there is limited research on how this model could be adapted to less centralised political systems.

- **New Zealand's Bicultural Education Initiatives:** Grounded in its commitment to Māori language and cultural preservation, New Zealand's policies provide valuable insights into balancing cultural revival with inclusivity for immigrant populations.

- **South Korea's Cultural Globalisation:** As a leader in cultural exports through K-pop and K-dramas, South Korea has built significant cultural capital. A study on how Cultural Education ties into its soft power strategy could offer new perspectives.

The Role of Australia in Global Research

Australia's position as a multicultural hub provides a unique platform for leading global research. Initiatives such as the VMC could broaden their scope to assess the long-term impact of funding allocation, ensuring that it develops societal cohesion rather than isolationist tendencies. Moreover, integrating Cultural Education into national surveys and reports, such as the Australian Bureau of Statistics (2024), could provide critical longitudinal data to track changes in inclusivity.

Conclusion
Cultural Education and CQ

A Blueprint for a Resilient World

This book represents more than an exploration of Cultural Education; it is a call to action, a blueprint for transformative change, and a vision for a future where humanity flourishes through understanding, respect, and shared purpose. In a world fractured by division, inequality, and escalating conflicts, Cultural Education and **Cultural Intelligence (CQ)** offer a beacon of hope - a means to dismantle prejudices, celebrate diversity, and build bridges across cultures.

A Vision for the Future

Imagine a society where schools are sanctuaries of understanding, workplaces thrive on inclusive innovation, and governments legislate with a profound respect for the richness of human diversity. Picture a future where every child grows up with the tools to challenge stereotypes, every adult has the opportunity to confront and overcome biases, and every institution embodies the principles of equity and respect.

This is the future that **Cultural Education and CQ** can create - a world where diversity is not a challenge to be managed but a strength to be celebrated. It is a future where cultural literacy and CQ are as foundational as reading and mathematics, where inclusivity shapes not only policies but everyday interactions, and where communities unite to face shared challenges with empathy and collaboration.

Cultural Education: Transformative Tools for Change

Throughout this book, we have framed **Cultural Education** as the structured pathway for building **Cultural Intelligence (CQ)** - the ability to navigate and engage with cultural diversity effectively. CQ provides the skills, awareness, and responsiveness to apply the values of empathy, respect, and inclusion across all facets of life. Together, Cultural Education and CQ empower individuals, institutions, and societies to break down barriers, foster mutual understanding, and thrive in a globalised world.

Planting the Seeds of Change

Change begins with small, deliberate steps. Here are ways individuals, institutions, and governments can begin embedding Cultural Education into the fabric of society:

1. **Individuals**: Begin with self-reflection. Identify your biases, question your assumptions, and actively seek out perspectives different from your own. Engage in conversations that challenge and expand your understanding, and practice empathy in your daily interactions.

2. **Educators**: Integrate Cultural Education and CQ principles into curricula at all levels. Create classrooms that hold space for diverse voices and experiences, where every student feels seen and valued. Equip yourself with the tools to teach inclusively and foster critical thinking about cultural identities and histories.

3. **Businesses and Organisations**: Adopt Cultural Intelligence as a core competency. Develop

diversity, equity, and inclusion (DEI) programs that go beyond symbolic gestures to drive meaningful change. Offer training that empowers employees to navigate cultural diversity with sensitivity and respect.

4. **Policymakers**: Legislate with Cultural Education and CQ in mind. Design policies that celebrate diversity, address systemic inequities, and create opportunities for marginalised communities. Ensure public institutions - schools, healthcare, law enforcement - reflect and respect the multicultural realities they serve.

5. **Communities**: Celebrate diversity through cultural festivals, storytelling initiatives, and intercultural dialogue. Build spaces where people from different backgrounds can connect, share, and learn from one another, fostering a sense of collective belonging.

The Promise of Cultural Intelligence

While writing this book, a broader vision emerged: the integration of **Cultural Intelligence (CQ)** into every aspect of society. Imagine a future where CQ is a recognised skillset as essential as literacy or numeracy, where it underpins decisions in education, business, governance, and community building. By embedding CQ into public consciousness, we can create systems that not only recognise diversity but actively thrive on it.

A Call to Action

The time to act is now. The world is not merely changing - it is demanding change. The rise of nationalism, the persistence of systemic inequalities, and the erosion of social cohesion call for bold, collective action. Cultural Education is not just solutions; it is the foundation for a fairer, more harmonious world.

- **To educators**: Teach beyond textbooks. Bring the richness of the world's cultures into your classrooms, and empower students to think critically about the world they will inherit.

- **To policymakers**: Prioritise Cultural Education in national curricula and public initiatives. Treat it as investments in societal resilience and progress.

- **To business leaders**: Recognise that diversity drives innovation. Make CQ a cornerstone of your corporate strategies.

- **To individuals**: Lead by example. Be the change you wish to see in your family, your workplace, and your community.

A Future Worth Striving For

The world is becoming smaller, more interconnected, and more complex. The challenges we face - climate change, political polarisation, economic inequities - require solutions rooted in collaboration and mutual respect. Cultural Education and CQ are not just tools for navigating these challenges; they are transformative forces that can shape a world where humanity thrives together.

This book is both a guide and a starting point. Its pages carry a message of hope, a vision for change, and a roadmap for action. As you close this book, consider the role you can play in this journey. How will you contribute to a society that values diversity, nurtures empathy, and builds bridges of understanding?

The future is unwritten, but the seeds of Cultural Education and CQ have been planted. Together, we can cultivate a world where every individual feels valued, every voice is heard, and every culture is celebrated. This is not merely a dream - it is a promise. Let us begin.

Bibliography

Acemoglu, D, Gelb, S & Robinson, J 2007, *Black Economic Empowerment and economic performance in South Africa*, Massachusetts Institute of Technology, Department of Economics, viewed 5 December 2024, https://www.treasury.gov.za/publications/other/growth/06-procurement%20and%20bee/02-black%20economic%20empowerment%20and%20economic%20performance%20in%20so.pdf.

American Psychological Association (APA) 2010, *Parental influence on diversity attitudes*, viewed 1 December 2024, https://apa.org.

Ashton, K 2024, 'Suburban candidate campaign sign targeted with racist vandalism ahead of Victorian council elections', *Australian Broadcasting Corporation (ABC)*, 26 September, viewed 1 December 2024, https://www.abc.net.au/news/2024-09-26/jamel-singh-casey-council-candidate-racist-vandalism/104396874.

Attwood, B 2005, *Telling the Truth About Aboriginal History*, Allen & Unwin Book Publishers, Sydney, Australia.

Australian Bureau of Statistics (ABS) 2024, *Migrant settlement outcomes*, viewed 13 December 2024, https://www.abs.gov.au/statistics/people/people-and-communities/migrant-settlement-outcomes/latest-release.

Australian Bureau of Statistics (ABS) 2024, *Youth offenders: 2022–23 financial year*, viewed 1 December 2024, https://www.abs.gov.au/statistics/people/crime-and-justice/recorded-crime-offenders/latest-release.

Australian Curriculum Assessment and Reporting Authority (ACARA) 2023, *Australian curriculum review*, viewed 1 December 2024, https://acara.edu.au/docs/default-source/curriculum/review-of-f-10-australian-curriculum.pdf?sfvrsn=60e27007_4.

Australian Curriculum Assessment and Reporting Authority (ACARA) 2023, *Cross-curriculum priorities (Version 8.4)*, viewed 1 December 2024, https://www.australiancurriculum.edu.au/f-10-curriculum/cross-curriculum-priorities/.

Australian Government 2024, *Australian Institute of Criminology - Annual Report 2023-24*, viewed 5 December 2024, https://www.aic.gov.au/sites/default/files/2024-10/aic_annual_report_2023-24.pdf.

Australian Institute of Aboriginal and Torres Strait Islander Studies (AIATSIS) 2023, *First Nations peoples and cultures*, viewed 1 December 2024, https://aiatsis.gov.au/search/content?key=First+Nations+peoples+and+cultures.

Avolio, BJ & Hannah, ST 2020, 'An enduring leadership myth: Born a leader or made a leader?', *Organizational Dynamics*, vol. 49, no. 4, pp. 1–8.

The Aziz Foundation (Aziz) 2024, *Institutionalised: The rise of Islamophobia in higher education*, viewed 1 December 2024, https://www.azizfoundation.org.uk/resources/.

Barton, C, Gonzales, M & Ward, T 2015, *Restorative justice practices in schools: A review*, Springer, New York.

Beyond Blue 2021, *First Nations mental health*, viewed 1 December 2024, https://beyondblue.org.au.

Beyond Blue 2023, *Mental health and bullying in Australian schools*, viewed 1 December 2024, https://beyondblue.org.au.

Barton, C, Gonzales, M & Ward, T 2015, *Restorative justice practices in schools: A review*, Springer, New York.

Bennett, B & Morse, C unpub., Continuous Improvement Cultural Responsiveness Tools (CICRT): Creating More Culturally Responsive Social Workers, Federation University, viewed 1 December 2024, https://www.tandfonline.com/doi/pdf/10.1080/0312407X.2023.2186255?needAccess=true.

Boerma, M, Coyle, EA, Dietrich, MA, Dintzner, MR, Drayton, SJ, Early, JL, Edginton, AN, Horlen, CK, Kirkwood, CK, Lin, AYF, Rager, ML, Shah-Manek, B, Welch, AC & Williams, NT 2017, 'Point/Counterpoint: Are outstanding leaders born or made?', *American Journal of Pharmaceutical Education*, vol. 81, no. 3, pp. 2–4.

British Broadcasting Corporation (BBC) 2021, 'Cultural awareness in homogenous communities', viewed 1 December 2024, https://bbc.com.

Bureau Report 2024, 'Locals launch petition against government's decision to rename Melbourne's lake after Guru Nanak Dev Ji', *The Australia Today*, 16 November, viewed 1 December 2024, https://www.theaustraliatoday.com.au/locals-launch-petition-against-governments-decision-to-rename-melbournes-lake-after-guru-nanak-dev-ji/.

Catalyst 2021, *Gender diversity on boards in Norway*, viewed 1 December 2024, https://catalyst.org.

Centre for Peace and Conflict Studies (CPCS) 2022, 'African research on cultural dialogue and potential outcomes', viewed 5 December 2024, https://www.centrepeaceconflictstudies.org/.

Charter, D 2024, 'WWE boss Linda McMahon to lead Trump's vision of 'patriotic' education', *The Times,* 20 November, viewed 5 December 2024, https://www.thetimes.com/world/us-world/article/linda-mcmahon-education-secretary-trump-wwe-wrestling-k7z6qxhsg.

Commonwealth Bank of Australia (CBA) 2023, *Annual report: Diversity and inclusion initiatives*, viewed 1 December 2024, https://commbank.com.au.

Commonwealth Bank of Australia (CBA) 2023, *Diversity and inclusion report*, viewed 1 December 2024, https://commbank.com.au.

Commonwealth of Australia (2008), *National Apology to the Stolen Generations*, viewed 1 December 2024, https://www.aph.gov.au/Visit_Parliament/Art/Icons/Apology_to_Australias_Indigenous_Peoples.

Cultural Infusion (2024), *Diversity Atlas*, viewed 5 December 2024, from https://diversityatlas.io/.

Deloitte 2021, *The diversity and inclusion revolution*, viewed 1 December 2024, https://deloitte.com.

Department of Education, Skills, and Employment (DOE) 2023, *Cultural Education and National Curriculum: A Framework for Inclusion*, viewed 1 December 2024, https://www.education.gov.au/australian-curriculum.

Department of Education, Skills and Employment (DOE) 2022, *Harmony Day in schools*, viewed 1 December 2024, https://education.gov.au.

Deutsche Welle 2019, *Refugee integration in Germany*, viewed 1 December 2024, https://dw.com.

Diversity Council Australia (DCA) 2022, *Inclusion at work index*, viewed 1 December 2024, https://dca.org.au.

Driskell, J, Copper, C, & Moran, A 1994, 'Does mental practice enhance performance?' *Journal of Applied Psychology*, vol. 79(4), pp. 481–492, https://doi.org/10.1037/0021-9010.79.4.48.

Edmondson, A 2024, 'PSYCHOLOGICAL SAFETY & FAILING WELL with Harvard Business School Professor Amy Edmondson', *Talk About Talk*, podcast, viewed 5 December 2024, https://www.talkabouttalk.com/amy-edmondson-175/.

Embrace Equity 2024, *Empower your team with Anti-Racism Leadership Development*, viewed 1 December 2024, https://www.embracingequity.org/post/empower-your-team-with-anti-racism-leadership-development?3e4ed96d_page=12.

Environics Institute 2020, *Canadian multiculturalism survey*, viewed 1 December 2024, https://environics.ca.

European Commission Against Racism and Intolerance (ECARI) 2021, *Cultural education in England*, viewed 1 December 2024, https://coe.int/ecri.

European Commission Against Racism and Intolerance (ECARI) 2021, *Laïcité and its impact on minority rights in France*, viewed 1 December 2024, https://coe.int/ecri.

European Commission Against Racism and Intolerance (ECARI) 2024, *Report on the United Kingdom*, viewed 1 December 2024, https://rm.coe.int/sixth-report-on-the-united-kingdom/1680b20bdc.

Finnish National Agency for Education (FNAE) 2021, *Multicultural education policies*, viewed 1 December 2024, https://oph.fi.

George, L, & Park, C 2016, 'Meaning in Life as Comprehension, Purpose, and Mattering: Toward Integration and New Research Questions', *Review of General Psychology*, vol. 20 no.3, pp. 205-220, viewed 7 December 2024, https://doi.org/10.1037/gpr0000077.

German Federal Office for Migration and Refugees (GFOMR) 2023, *Integration courses in Germany*, viewed 1 December 2024, https://bamf.de.

Gershoff, E 2016, *Corporal punishment and its long-term effects on children*, Sage Publications, Thousand Oaks, CA.

Gierszewska, W & Sinning, V 2023, 'Civic Education in Rwanda: the impact of the Itorero program', *Intercultural Education in Poland and Worldwide*, viewed 15 July 2024, https://doi.org/10.15804/em.2023.04.03.

GNH Centre Bhutan 2024, *GNH Happiness Index website*, viewed 14 August 2024, https://www.gnhcentrebhutan.org/gnh-happiness-index/.

Google Diversity Report (GDR) 2023, *Advancing representation and belonging*, viewed 1 December 2024, https://diversity.google.

GovTech and UNDP 2024, 'Kingdom of Bhutan: Digital Development and Transformation Strategy', *UNDP Bhutan*, 29 May, viewed 14 August 2024, https://www.undp.org/bhutan/publications/kingdom-bhutan-digital-development-and-transformation-strategy.

Hannaford, P 2024, 'An absolute joke': Victorian's Allan Government under fire for renaming Melbourne lake after 15th century Sikh religious figure', *Sky News Australia*, 13 November, viewed 14 November 2024, https://www.skynews.com.au/australia-news/an-absolute-joke-victorias-allan-government-under-fire-for-renaming-melbourne-lake-after-15th-century-sikh-religious-figure/news-story/d69475d8d8e2b4f1582316f9c1304abf.

Hill, P & Turiano, N 2014, 'Purpose in Life as a Predictor of Mortality Across Adulthood', *Psychological Science*, vol. 25, no. 7, pp. 1482-1486, viewed July 2024, https://doi.org/10.1177/0956797614531799.

Hillman, AL & Jenkner, E 2004, 'Educating Children in Poor Countries', *International Monetary Fund, Economic Issue*, vol. 33, viewed 5 December 2024, https://www.imf.org/external/pubs/ft/issues/issues33/.

Hunt, V, Prince, S, Dixon-Fyle, S & Dolan, K 2020, *Diversity wins: How inclusion matters*, viewed 1 December 2024, https://www.mckinsey.com/~/media/mckinsey/featured%20insights/diversity%20and%20inclusion/diversity%20wins%20how%20inclusion%20matters/diversity-wins-how-inclusion-matters-vf.pdf.

Hsu, T & Paton, E 2019, 'Gucci and Adidas Apologize and Drop Products Called Racist', *The New York Times*, 17 February, viewed 3 September 2024, https://www.nytimes.com/2019/02/07/business/gucci-blackface-adidas-apologize.html.

Journal of Adolescent Health (JAH) 2020, 'The psychological impact of exclusion', viewed 1 December 2024, https://jahonline.org.

Kerr, S 1975, 'On the folly of rewarding A, while hoping for B', *Academy of Management Journal*, vol. 18, no. 4, pp. 769–783.

Kemmerer, B & Arnold, V 1993, 'The growing use of benchmarking in managing cultural diversity', *Business forum,* vol. 18, no. 1-2, p. 38.

Locke, E, and Latham, G, 2015, 'Goal-setting theory', *In Organizational Behavior*, vol. 1, pp. 159-183, Routledge.

Mandalaywala, TM, Tai, C & Rhodes, M 2020, 'Children's use of race and gender as cues to social status', *National Library of Medicine,* PMC PubMed Central, viewed 6 July 2024, 10.1371/journal.pone.0234398.

Multidisciplinary Digital Publishing Institute (MDPI) 2022, 'Cultural Responsiveness in Education and its Role in Mitigating Bullying', *MDPI Journal of Education*, viewed 5 December 2024, https://www.mdpi.com/2227-9067/10/10/1632.

Ministry of Education, Culture, Sports, Science and Technology, Japan (MECSSTJ) 2023, *Cultural education policies in Japan*, viewed 1 December 2024, https://mext.go.jp.

Ministry of Education (MOE) 2014, *Bhutan Education Blueprint 2014-2024, Rethinking Education*, viewed 15 August 2024, http://www.education.gov.bt/?p=7669.

Morrison, A, Rigney, L-I, Hattam, R & Diplock, A 2019, *Toward an Australian Culturally Inclusive Pedagogy*, University of South Australia, viewed 1 December 2024, https://childrensa.sa.gov.au/wp-content/uploads/2023/03/Annex-3-Morrison-Rigney-Hattam-Diplock-2019.pdf.

National Library of Australia (NLA) 2023, *Willem Janszoon and early European exploration*, viewed 1 December 2024, https://nla.gov.au.

New Zealand Ministry of Education (NZME) 2023, *Māori language in schools*, viewed 1 December 2024, https://education.govt.nz.

Northouse, PG 2018, *Interactive: Leadership* (International Student Edition), 1st edn, SAGE Publications, USA.

Norwegians Ministries 2021, *Migration and Integration 2020-2021, Report for Norway to the OECD*, viewed 5 July 2024, https://kudos.dfo.no/documents/25921/files/23692.pdf.

OECD 2021, *Education at a Glance 2021: OECD Indicators*, OECD Publishing, Paris, viewed 5 July 2024, https://doi.org/10.1787/b35a14e5-en.

OECD 2021, *Education in Brazil: An International Perspective*, OECD Publishing, Paris, viewed 5 July 2024, https://doi.org/10.1787/60a667f7-en.

OECD 2024, *Bhutan's Gross National Happiness (GNH) Index*, OECD Publishing, viewed 14 August 2024, https://www.oecd.org/en/publications/well-being-knowledge-exchange-platform-kep_93d45d63-en/bhutan-s-gross-national-happiness-gnh-index_ff75e0a9-en.html.

Park, JY 2010, 'Reverse immigration (Studying and Immigration in Australia)', *QUT ePrints*, Korea, viewed 13 December 2024, https://eprints.qut.edu.au/39024/#:~:text=Reverse%20immigration%20refers%20to%20re,them%20before%20immigration%20to%20Australia.

Parker, K, Horowitz, JM & Anderson, M 2020, 'Amid protests, majorities across racial and ethnic groups express support for the Black Lives Matter movement', *Pew Research Centre*, viewed 1 December 2024, https://pewresearch.org/social-trends/2020/06/12/amid-protests-majorities-across-racial-and-ethnic-groups-express-support-for-the-black-lives-matter-movement.

Pew Research Center (PRC) 2024, *Cultural issues and the 2024 Elections*, viewed 1 December 2024, https://pewresearch.org.

Pew Research Center (PRC) 2022, *The impact of racial justice movements on education*, viewed 1 December 2024, https://pewresearch.org.

Porter, G 2004, 'Meeting the challenge: Inclusion and diversity in Canadian schools', *Education CANADA-TORONTO*, vol. 44(1), pp. 48-51, viewed 5 July 2024, https://www.researchgate.net/profile/Gordon-Porter/publication/228690547_Meeting_the_challenge_Inclusion_and_diversity_in_Canadian_schools/links/570579e208aef745f7176cdb/Meeting-the-challenge-Inclusion-and-diversity-in-Canadian-schools.pdf.

Reynolds, H 2006, *The Other Side of the Frontier: Aboriginal Resistance to the European Invasion of Australia*, UNSW Press, Australia.

Rodrigues-Hidalgo, AJ, Calmaestra, J, Casas, JA & Ortega-Ruiz, R 2019, 'Ethnic-Cultural Bullying Versus Personal Bullying: Specificity and Measurement of Discriminatory Aggression and Victimization Amoung Adolescents', *Frontiers in Psychology*, vol. 10, viewed 10 July 2024, https://doi.org/10.3389/fpsyg.2019.00046.

Roots of Empathy 2021, *Program impact report*, viewed 1 December 2024, https://rootsofempathy.org.

Samaritans of Singapore (SOS) 2021, *Singapore reported 452 suicide deaths in 2020, number of elderly suicide deaths highest recorded since 1991*, viewed 26 November 2024, https://www.sos.org.sg/pressroom/singapore-reported-452-suicide-deaths-in-2020-number-of-elderly-suicide-deaths-highest-recorded-since-1991/.

SAP Diversity Report 2022, *Autism at work program*, viewed 1 December 2024, https://sap.com.

Sapouna, M, de Amicis, L & Vezzali, L 2023, 'Bullying Victimization Due to Racial, Ethnic, Citizenship and/or Religious Status: A Systematic Review', *Adolescent Res Rev*, vol. 8, pp. 261–296, viewed 5 July 2024, https://doi.org/10.1007/s40894-022-00197-2https://link.springer.com/article/10.1007/s40894-022-00197-2.

SBS News 2013, 'Timeline: Australia's Immigration Policy', 21 June, viewed 1 December 2024, https://www.sbs.com.au/news/article/timeline-australias-immigration-policy/pc9vvzxd1.

Scroll in. 2023, 'Domestic Violence', viewed 6 July 2024, https://scroll.in/tag/domestic-violence.

Scanlon Foundation 2024, *2024 'Mapping Social Cohesion Report'*, *Scanlon Institute*, viewed 9 December 2024, https://scanloninstitute.org.au/publications/mapping-social-cohesion-report/2024-mapping-social-cohesion-report.

Schonert-Reichl, KA 2023, 'Encouraging advances in the science on mindfulness and compassion in schools: current research, lingering questions, and future directions', *Mindfulness*, vol. 14, no. 2, pp. 300-306, viewed 8 December 2024, https://link.springer.com/article/10.1007/s12671-023-02070-2.

Shanker, S 2016, *Self-reg: How to help your child (and you) break the stress cycle and successfully engage with life*, Penguin Canada, Toronto.

SHRM 2020, *Diversity and inclusion in the workplace*, viewed 1 December 2024, https://shrm.org.

Singh, D 2024, *The Zen of Sikhing*, published Amazon, Australia.

Singh, JK 2024, *The World is our Playground*, (Book 1-6) of the series, Amazon, Australia.

Smith, PJ 2024, *Cultural Responsiveness: A Conceptual Model for Mental Health Professionals Engaging with Aboriginal and Torres Strait Islander People*, Doctorate in Philosophy, University of New England, viewed 1 December 2024, https://hdl.handle.net/1959.11/57950.

Swedish Ministry of Education (SME) 2022, *Diversity education outcomes*, viewed 1 December 2024, https://skolverket.se.

Swedish National Agency for Education (SNAE) 2023, *Equality and diversity in schools*, viewed 1 December 2024, https://skolverket.se.

Taylor, S, Pham, L, Rivkin, I, & Armor, D 1998, 'Harnessing the imagination: Mental simulation, self-regulation, and coping', *American Psychologist*, vol. 53, no. 4, pp. 429–439, https://doi.org/10.1037/0003-066X.53.4.429.

Telstra 2023, *Annual sustainability report*, viewed 1 December 2024, https://telstra.com.au.

Umans, T, Smith, E, Anderson, W & Planken, W 2018, 'Top management teams' shared leadership and ambidexterity: The role of management control systems', *International Review of Administrative Sciences*, vol. 86, no. 3, pp. 444–462.

Telecommunications and Digital Government Regulatory Authority 2024, 'Tolerance initiatives', *United Arab Emirates (UAE)*, viewed 8 December 2024, https://u.ae/en/about-the-uae/culture/tolerance/tolerance-initiatives.

United Nations Education and Scientific Cultural Organisation (UNESCO) 2023, 'Prevention of violence and bullying in school', viewed 15 July 2024, https://www.unesco.org/gem-report/en/articles/prevention-violence-and-bullying-school.

United Nations High Commissioner for Refugees (UNHCR 2023), *Global Appeal*, viewed 1 December 2024, https://reporting.unhcr.org/globalappeal-2023#:~:text=2023%20Global%20planning%20figures&text=117.2%20million%20people%20will%20be,2023%2C%20according%20to%20UNHCR's%20estimations.

Vroom, V 1964, *Work and Motivation*, Jossey-Bass, San Francisco.

Wager, TD, Atlas, LY 2015, 'The neuroscience of placebo effects: connecting context, learning and health', *Nat Rev Neurosci*, vol. 16, no. 7, viewed 10 November 2024, https://pmc.ncbi.nlm.nih.gov/articles/PMC6013051/.

Weddle, B, Parsons, J and Howard, W 2024, 'Five bold moves to quickly transform you organization's culture', *McKinsey & Company*, viewed 1 December 2024, https://www.mckinsey.com/capabilities/people-and-organizational-performance/our-insights/five-bold-moves-to-quickly-transform-your-organizations-culture.

Wilson, E 2014, 'Diversity, culture and the glass ceiling', *Journal of Cultural Diversity*, vol. 21, no. 3, pp. 83–89.

Workplace Gender Equality Agency (WGEA) 2023, *Australia's gender pay gap statistics*, viewed 2 December 2024, https://wgea.gov.au.

Wynne, E 2018, 'Sikh Australians and their contributions celebrated in new Perth monument', *ABC News*, 20 April, viewed 10 December 2024, https://www.abc.net.au/news/2018-04-20/trail-of-sikh-australian-stories-celebrated/9672780.

Yallop, R and Yosufzai, R 2024, 'Why Australian attitudes on religion and immigration have hardened, but social cohesion is stable', *SBS News*, 19 November, viewed 1 December 2024, https://sbs.com.au/news/article/why-australian-attitudes-on-religion-and-immigration-have-hardened-but-social-cohesion-is-stable/hp1bxaf4c.

About the Author

Dr Jamel Kaur Singh is a passionate advocate for Cultural Intelligence (CQ) & Cultural Education with over three decades of experience across diverse sectors, including education, real estate, the Australian Defence Force, finance, First Nations advocacy, interfaith dialogue, multicultural integration, and community engagement. She recently earned her doctorate in Business Administration at Edmonton University (2025) after completing her MBA with the Australian Institute of Business. Born in the United Kingdom to Malaysian-born Sikh parents, world-renowned artist and author, Dya Singh and interfaith advocate, Jessiee Kaur Singh, and raised in Australia since the age of four, her life bridges Eastern and Western cultural narratives, providing her with a unique perspective on promoting inclusivity.

As an educator, author, and consultant, her work includes *The World is Our Playground* book series, cultural workshops, teacher Professional Development, and corporate training initiatives designed to eliminate biases and celebrate diversity. As a visionary businesswoman, she has built her own eclectic workforce that reflects her strong commitment to unity with diversity, connectedness, and inclusion. This book is the culmination of a deeply personal and professional journey, inspired by the desire to address systemic gaps in cultural awareness across education, policy, and corporate practices.